D0710778

SPIRITUAL WARFARE

FOR THE END TIMES

.

SPIRITUAL WARFARE

FOR THE END TIMES

HOW TO DEFEAT THE ENEMY

DEREK PRINCE

Chosen

a division of Baker Publishing Group
Minneapolis, Minnesota

© 2017 by Derek Prince Ministries

Published by Chosen Books
11400 Hampshire Avenue South
Minneapolis, Minnesota 55438
www.chosenbooks.com

Chosen Books is a division of
Baker Publishing Group, Grand Rapids, Michigan

Printed in the United States of America

All rights reserved. No part of this publication may be reproduced, stored in a retrieval system, or transmitted in any form or by any means—for example, electronic, photocopy, recording—without the prior written permission of the publisher. The only exception is brief quotations in printed reviews.

Library of Congress Cataloging-in-Publication Data
Names: Prince, Derek, author.
Title: Spiritual warfare for the end times : how to defeat the enemy / Derek Prince.
Description: Minneapolis, Minnesota : Chosen, 2017. | Includes index.
Identifiers: LCCN 2016059956 | ISBN 9780800798208 (trade paper : alk. paper)
Subjects: LCSH: Spiritual warfare.
Classification: LCC BV4509.5 .P754 2017 | DDC 235/.4—dc23
LC record available at https://lccn.loc.gov/2016059956

Unless otherwise indicated, Scripture quotations are from the New King James Version®. Copyright © 1982 by Thomas Nelson, Inc. Used by permission. All rights reserved.

Scripture quotations identified NASB are from the New American Standard Bible®, copyright © 1960, 1962, 1963, 1968, 1971, 1972, 1973, 1975, 1977, 1995 by The Lockman Foundation. Used by permission. (www.Lockman.org)

Scripture quotations identified *The Living Bible* are from The Living Bible, copyright © 1971. Used by permission of Tyndale House Publishers, Inc., Carol Stream, Illinois 60188. All rights reserved.

Scripture quotations identified KJV are from the King James Version of the Bible.

Cover design by Brian Bobel

Baker Publishing Group publications use paper produced from sustainable forestry practices and post-consumer waste whenever possible.

23   24   25   26   27   28   12   11   10   9   8   7

Contents

Preface

Spiritual Warfare for the End Times

Most people believe that evil is a *what*. But in reality, evil is a *who*. Unless you face this truth, you and your family may end up being victims of that evil.

At this moment in history, we are witnessing an unprecedented escalation of malevolence that is sending shock waves around the world. People of all faiths are wondering if these events are a sign of the beginning of the close of this age.

The truth we must face is that *someone*—our adversary, the devil—is out to deceive, destabilize and destroy the peoples and nations of the world. As Christians we know there is something the Church is supposed to be doing about all this. The question is, *What? How do we fight this enemy? How do we win this war?*

Although these are perilous times, you and I have nothing to fear. There are answers—and some of them can be found in this powerful and timely book by Derek Prince, *Spiritual Warfare for the End Times*.

Derek pulls no punches. Instead he pulls back the curtain the evil one has been hiding behind. In this book he outlines *exactly* what the Church needs to do, and how to do it.

In one of the opening chapters Derek makes the following statement:

> Here is my belief: The devil wants to keep us in the dark. If there is one truth that the devil wants to keep us from knowing, it is that we have the authority to bring his kingdom to an end. Until we know it, we will not do it. But when we know it, we must determine to do it.

These statements encapsulate the purpose of this landmark volume. By the time you finish reading *Spiritual Warfare for the End Times*, you will know beyond all doubt that we have the authority and power to bring Satan's kingdom to an end.

In this volume we have the benefit of sixty years of Derek Prince's expertise in spiritual warfare, condensed into a compelling page-turner you will not want to put down. From the first pages, you will realize that you have entered an extraordinary training ground to become the spiritual champion you were meant to be.

At Derek Prince Ministries, we believe this book will play a pivotal role in bringing the Church to her full stature. What will be the result? Christians will move closer and closer to the tipping point of victory in the battle against the enemy of our souls. Ultimately, by the word of our testimony and the blood of the Lamb, not loving our lives unto death, you and I will pull the kingdom of Satan down once and for all.

Our hope for this book is that it will help us achieve that great and final victory in the name of our Lord Jesus Christ. This is our commission—and it is our destiny in Him.

The International Publishing Team
of Derek Prince Ministries

Introduction

How to Overcome Evil

There is evil in our world. Would you agree? I believe that the presence of evil in the world is an almost universally acknowledged truth. In present day society, it has become fashionable to call evil by different, more socially acceptable names. The tendency has become to attribute its presence to a variety of social, cultural and psychological dynamics. If we believe the Bible, however, we must agree that there is a dark, aggressive force at work in our world that can only be described as "evil."

Some Christians believe that evil is an unstoppable force. They have resigned themselves to the fact that evil will eventually overcome the world and will only be defeated by the intervention of Jesus' return to the earth. In contrast to that approach, other Christians believe that if the Church would simply pray harder, or if we could institute more evangelism and political activism, we could eventually bring the Kingdom of God to the earth. Though there may be some elements of truth in each of these viewpoints, neither gives us an accurate picture of what the Bible has to say about the evil in our world. Nor does either viewpoint recognize or explain how God has called us to be active participants in this cosmic conflict.

Every day, you and I are confronted by the presence and the power of evil in various forms—sometimes from our environment and culture, and sometimes from within our own hearts and minds. As much as we hate to admit it, we do not always succeed in overcoming these forces of evil—not because we do not want to, but because we often do not know how to. Through this book I hope, by examination of Scripture, to help us discover the all-important "how to." I intend to outline how you and I can actually overcome evil.

Our first step in approaching this important subject is to recognize that there is no room for neutrality in our struggle against evil. There are two, and only two, alternatives: Either we overcome evil or we are overcome by it.

In Romans 12:21, Paul presented these alternatives very concisely when he wrote: "Do not be overcome by evil, but overcome evil with good." We see here that Paul gives us just two choices: Either we overcome evil, or evil will overcome us. There is no state of neutrality where we can refuse to deal with evil and still not be overcome by it.

What was Paul's plan of action? "Overcome evil with good." It is important to see that there is only one power in the universe strong enough to overcome evil—and that is good. We must meet every evil with a good that is more powerful than the evil that confronts us.

What is the only source of such goodness? God Himself.

Here is our conclusion, based upon the following string of logical statements. In order to overcome evil, you and I must be alive in God—having access to God's resources, wisdom, power and the weapons He has placed at our disposal. The goodness of God and all the resources that flow from His goodness are not only revealed to us but also made available through God's Word. In order to overcome evil, we must be acquainted with the Bible. We must know what the Bible teaches about evil. We must also know the provision God has made for us to overcome that evil.

What I have just outlined in these statements is the purpose of this book.

.

1

Evil Is Someone

We begin this first chapter with two clear statements in our minds. First, there is evil in the world. Second, we have a biblical mandate as Christians to overcome this evil. As we confront evil and look to the Bible for guidance and wisdom, we find one specific revelation in God's Word that is a key to the entirety of our conflict with evil. If we do not grasp this key and use it, we will be continually frustrated and ultimately defeated.

Here is that key: *Evil is not something; it is someone.*

I remember when this revelation came to me and the consequent transformation it brought. As a young preacher I wrestled for years with depression. I was a committed Christian, actively involved in ministry, yet still facing severe bouts with depression. I used every means I knew to overcome it—I prayed, fasted, studied the Bible and made resolutions—all to little or no avail. The depression only got worse.

I was desperate. But then a life-changing revelation came from Isaiah 61:3. This is the passage where the Lord speaks of what He will do for His people, promising "to give them beauty for ashes, the oil of joy for mourning, the garment of praise for the *spirit of heaviness*" (emphasis added). When I read the phrase *the spirit of heaviness*, by revelation I suddenly saw that my problem was *a person*. Even though it was an invisible spirit without a body, it was still a very real person. A *spirit* of heaviness, or depression, was systematically attacking me.

The powerful oppressor who had been seeking to destroy me and to ruin my ministry had been exposed. That evil was not *something*; it was *someone*—and the time had come for me to overcome him.

With this realization, I was 80 percent of the way to victory. Then I remembered that this was a family problem. My father, and probably his father, had fought this very same battle for years.

To gain complete victory over that awful spirit of depression, I needed only one other Scripture: "It shall come to pass, that whosoever shall call on the name of the LORD shall be delivered" (Joel 2:32 KJV). When I called on the Lord specifically to be delivered from the spirit of heaviness, in the name of the Lord Jesus Christ, quoting Joel 2:32, I was delivered!

This principle of evil as a person, not a thing, is consistent with the whole revelation of Scripture. Behind all evil, there is a person whom the Bible identifies by two primary names. In the Old Testament he is called *Satan*, and in the New Testament he is identified as *the devil*. Each name has a significant meaning.

The title *Satan* means "the one who resists or opposes." He is the one who resists and opposes God, God's purposes and God's people. As the people of God, we must recognize that Satan, acting as the adversary or the resister, opposes us.

The New Testament title *the devil* means "the slanderer" or "the accuser." Why is this name so appropriate? Because the main weapon Satan uses against us is accusation.

The Rival Kingdom

Where did this adversary of ours come from and when did this battle begin? Though his origin is a profound question, the Word of God does show us that at his creation Satan was not Satan as we know him presently. He was Lucifer, one of the chief archangels of God, outstanding both for his beauty and his wisdom. Apparently he was in charge of one third of all the created angels.

Because of Lucifer's great beauty and wisdom, however, his heart became proud, and he determined to seek equality with God. (Most Bible scholars base this on Isaiah 14:12–15 and Ezekiel 28:13–17.) As a result of this determination to elevate himself, Lucifer rebelled and led the angels in his charge in a rebellion against Almighty God. As punishment for this insurrection, Lucifer and those angels were cast down from the heaven of God's dwelling.

Following his ejection from heaven, Lucifer (now Satan, the opposer) set up his own rival kingdom in another area of the universe—what the Bible refers to as "the heavenlies" or sometimes "the mid-heaven." The heavenlies are situated somewhere between earth and the heaven of God's throne—and they are the location of Satan's headquarters in this age. In the heavenlies he rules over the large company of rebellious angels. His supreme purpose is to resist and thwart God's purposes and God's people, primarily through slander and accusation. We will explore this in depth in the next chapter, along with several other key tactics.

Persons without Bodies

The New Testament presents insights on the location and operation of Satan's rival kingdom, as well as the spiritual beings operating with him. One of the clearest pictures is given to us by Paul in Ephesians 6:12: "For we do not wrestle against flesh and blood, but against principalities, against powers, against the rulers of the darkness of this age, against spiritual hosts of wickedness in the heavenly places."

Notice that there are spiritual forces of evil who not only have authority, but also seek to exercise that authority to dominate and rule. The following translation of this verse from *The Living Bible* provides helpful insights:

> For we are not fighting against people made of flesh and blood, but against persons without bodies—the evil rulers of the unseen world, those mighty satanic beings and great evil princes of darkness who rule this world; and against huge numbers of wicked spirits in the spirit world.

Notice the phrase *persons without bodies*. These evil spirit beings, including the devil, are in opposition to God and His people. They are located in the spirit world. This defines the nature of our warfare and the conflict in which we are engaged. Unless we understand this, we cannot possibly be fully successful engaging in this battle.

Thus, we can conclude four key points from Paul's statement as we begin our study of spiritual warfare for the end times. First, our conflict is cosmic. In other words, it involves the whole universe—not just earth, but heaven and earth.

Second, our battle is not in the realm of the senses. We do not discern the nature of our conflict by what we see or hear. Rather, we come to understand it by revelation from the Holy Spirit and out of our understanding of Scripture.

Third, this conflict and its nature are unrecognized by the majority of people. They are simply unaware of whom they are up against. They know they are struggling against something with significant force, but they cannot see it, understand it or define it. As a result, they do not know how to deal with it.

Finally, the outcome of this conflict is ultimately decisive for each one of us. The result in the spirit realm—whether it is victory or defeat—will determine the result in every other area of our lives.

2

How Satan Works

Understanding that evil is not *something* but *someone* is a vital weapon for warfare in the spiritual realm. Knowing this, we can begin to understand and counter some of Satan's most successful tactics against us. Let's begin by looking at several pictures in Scripture that help us visualize this enemy.

A Dragon/Serpent

Revelation 12:9 gives us this description: "The great dragon was cast out, that serpent of old, called the Devil and Satan, who deceives the whole world."

Here are two pictures of Satan: the dragon and the serpent. The dragon is a great, powerful, raging beast that inspires fear. At one point in my life I inherited from family members some antique porcelain vessels that were decorated with Chinese dragons. Ultimately, I decided not to keep those vessels because I did not want a portrait of Satan displayed continually in my home. The dragon is large, fearful, fierce and awe-inspiring. It threatens, terrifies, tramples and destroys.

The serpent or snake, on the other hand, is small and sometimes scarcely visible. Snakes do not operate in the same way as dragons. They slither quietly and can insert themselves through any little crack or hole. I was born in India and lived there until I was five years of age. One of the problems our family faced was the cobra. In fact, several thousand people die every year of snakebites in India. The cobra does not attack directly as a dragon does. Instead it comes up a bathroom pipe or through a small hole. Before you know it, the cobra is in the room with you ready to strike.

Satan can operate as a dragon, or he can behave like a snake. He can be large, fierce and terrifying, or he can be subtle and slippery—coming in through some little hole where you would least expect something dangerous to enter.

A Thieving Destroyer

Jesus gave us another picture of Satan: "The thief does not come except to steal, and to kill, and to destroy. I have come that they may have life, and that they may have it more abundantly" (John 10:10).

The thief here is the person of Satan. That role is contrasted clearly with Jesus' role: Satan is the life-taker; Jesus is the life-giver. Satan will usually disguise his motives and seek to conceal his presence and his activity, but his ultimate objectives never change. His intention is always to steal, to kill and to destroy.

To steal is to take away that which is rightfully ours. That refers specifically to our inheritance in God and the blessings God wants us to have. *To kill* refers to Satan's efforts to destroy our lives physically, whether directly or through sickness. Satan is a murderer. Indeed he is the source of all murder, war and genocide. *To destroy* (Greek, *apolese*) goes beyond time into eternity. This refers to the ultimate, ongoing, eternal destruction of the lost soul who has been deceived and ensnared by Satan. Always bear in mind this stark warning from Jesus.

Four Tactics He Uses

With these pictures of Satan as a dragon, serpent and thief presented in Scripture, we can begin to discern some of the main tactics he uses in warfare against us.

Accusation

We noted that the New Testament calls this enemy "the devil" or "the accuser/slanderer." This is the most common and constant activity of Satan, as portrayed in Revelation 12:10: "For the accuser of our brethren, who accused them before our God day and night, has been cast down."

Satan is continually misrepresenting us. He not only accuses us before God—he accuses us to ourselves. He magnifies all our bad points and overlooks our good ones, whispering everything bad that can be said against us in an effort to make us feel guilty, shameful or unworthy.

This is why accusation is Satan's greatest single tactic. If he can keep us feeling guilty, then we are never a match for him. We will never rise up, take the offensive and defeat him. (Later we will examine the Scriptural weapons God has provided for us to deal with Satan's accusations of guilt.)

Deception

The next tactic comes at the end of the passage we cited earlier in Revelation 12:9: "The great dragon was cast out, that serpent of old, called the Devil and Satan, who deceives the whole world." Jesus explained that Satan "does not stand in the truth because there is no truth in him. Whenever he speaks a lie, he speaks from his own nature, for he is a liar and the father of lies" (John 8:44 NASB).

Deception is a main tactic against us: Satan "deceives the whole world." Because he is a liar, he does not come to us with truth. He does not present facts. Why does this accomplish his purposes so well? Because once he has deceived and ensnared us, he can go on to his other evil deeds.

The only real safeguard against deception is the Word of God. Scripture is absolutely true. If we can be persuaded to believe something contrary to Scripture, we know that— somehow—behind that persuasion is the enemy. He is always working to twist our minds from scriptural beliefs and introduce deception to us. His aim in deceiving us is to destroy us.

Temptation

Here is how Matthew 4:3, a verse in the account of the temptation of Jesus by Satan in the wilderness, refers to Satan: "Now when the tempter came to Him, he said, 'If You are the Son of God, command that these stones become bread.'"

To tempt is "to entice." Satan entices us to do evil. He places before us something that is wrong or evil, yet he presents it as desirable or attractive. Once we become convinced it is indeed desirable and attractive, then Satan says, "If you want this, then here is what you need to do." Without exception, whatever Satan tries to persuade us to do is something that entails disobedience to God.

Hindrance

In Paul's letter to the believers in Thessalonica he says: "We wanted to come to you—even I, Paul, time and again—but Satan hindered us" (1 Thessalonians 2:18).

Hindering is another typical activity of Satan, especially toward the servants of God who are seeking to do God's will. Satan thwarts, resists and opposes our intentions by putting obstacles in our way and bringing opposition and confusion.

We see, then, four key ways in which Satan operates: He accuses, he deceives, he tempts (or entices) and he hinders. These are, of course, not the only ways the enemy opposes us, but they represent the most common tactics he uses—ones with which we will most often have to contend as we engage in warfare against him.

3

A Defeated Foe

Behind everything Satan does, he has one ultimate purpose: to steal, to kill and to destroy. Yet we know that we are called upon as believers to defeat the one who opposes us. What is the basis for our victory over him?

In this warfare, which is both personal and cosmic, there is one scriptural fact that alone makes it possible for us to overcome evil. Here is that fact: *Jesus has already defeated Satan on our behalf.* The victory over Satan is not waiting to be won. *It has been won.* It was won when Jesus died, shed His blood on the cross, was buried and rose again from the dead. This is the Good News—the Gospel—for us as individuals and for the entire human race. The victory Jesus won over Satan was total, permanent and irreversible.

Satan cannot change what has been accomplished by the cross. It is eternal, settled for all time by God. The enemy's only option, then, is to obscure the work of the cross—to keep God's people from realizing what has been accomplished for us at Calvary. Satan does everything he can to keep us from knowing, understanding and applying the victory Jesus has won.

A Victory Won

The truth of Jesus' conquest is portrayed in Colossians 2:13–15:

> And you, being dead in your trespasses and the uncircumcision of your flesh, He has made alive together with Him, having forgiven you all trespasses, having wiped out the handwriting of requirements that was against us, which was contrary to us. And He has taken it out of the way, having nailed it to the cross. Having disarmed principalities and powers, He made a public spectacle of them, triumphing over them in it.

This passage describes what God, the Father, did through Jesus Christ, the Son. At the cross, Christ disarmed all of Satan's forces, stripping them of their weapons and defeating them. Jesus did not merely defeat them; He triumphed over them—making a public spectacle of them. A "triumph" in the time of the Roman Empire was not just winning a victory; it was also a public demonstration and celebration of that victory. The defeated enemies were led in chains as captives behind the triumphal general's chariot for all to see.

When Jesus defeated Satan and all his evil forces at the cross, He stripped them of their weapons. Then He went one step further, putting them to shame by making a public spectacle of them. We cannot fully understand how Jesus did this unless we recognize what took place at the cross.

Freedom from Guilt

Through His death on the cross, Jesus nullified Satan's strongest weapon against us: guilt. Though Satan still accuses and slanders us, and still finds guilt a very successful tactic, Jesus actually dealt with the basis of our guilt in two ways.

First, through the cross all our sins are forgiven. Second, at the cross God cancelled the written code, the Law, with its regulations that stood opposed to us. We could never legitimately approach God, because we could never meet the requirements of the Law for righteousness. At the cross, however, God Himself took that restriction out of the way by nailing the Law in its entirety to the cross. When Jesus died on our behalf as our representative, He paid the final penalty for all who have broken the Law—the death penalty. With that final penalty paid, we are no longer subject to the requirements of the Law or guilt for our failure to keep it.

Jesus made it possible for us to be set free from guilt. He offers us forgiveness, and He has removed the requirement for us to observe the Law as a means to achieving righteousness with God. Instead, we now come to God on the basis of our faith in the death of Jesus—and that faith is credited to us as righteousness.

Deliverance from Darkness

Not only are we freed from guilt, but we are offered other benefits as well. Look at a further result of Jesus' work on the cross.

> [We give] thanks to the Father who has qualified us to be partakers of the inheritance of the saints in the light. He has delivered us from the power of darkness and conveyed us into the kingdom of the Son of His love, in whom we have redemption through His blood, the forgiveness of sins.
>
> Colossians 1:12–14

Every benefit of salvation centers on our redemption through the cross. Through that redemption, God has not only provided forgiveness of sins and release from the requirements of the Law, but has also rescued us. God has delivered us from the dominion of darkness. He has brought us into the Kingdom of His Son.

Please take note of a truth in these last statements: Darkness has dominion. It is a real kingdom. Never believe that Satan does not have power, because he does. His power came initially from God, who is the only source of power. But in his wickedness and rebellion, Satan has turned his power against God and against God's people.

Through the death of Jesus on the cross, however, a total transition of kingdoms has been provided for us. We have been delivered from the evil dominion of darkness. Once delivered, we have then been brought into the Kingdom of light. Since we are now citizens of God's Kingdom, He sends us as His representatives to administer the victory of Jesus over Satan. Jesus won the victory, but God leaves it to us, through faith, to understand the victory Jesus won and to administer it. Because we now have the authority of God's Kingdom vested in us, we may exercise authority over Satan and his works. We are empowered to overcome evil.

Exercising His Authority

Scripture records an incident that is perhaps the first time the Kingdom authority of Jesus was administered by His followers on a major scale. The event takes place in Luke 10:17–19:

> Then the seventy returned with joy, saying, "Lord, even the demons are subject to us in Your name." And He said to them, "I saw Satan fall like lightning from heaven. Behold, I give you the authority to trample on serpents and scorpions,

and over all the power of the enemy, and nothing shall by any means hurt you."

Jesus said that their use of Kingdom authority was like Satan falling from heaven as lightning. The disciples discovered to their intense joy that when they went out as the representatives of Jesus, exercising His authority, the evil spirits had to obey them in the name of Jesus.

The New Testament depicts Jesus and His followers confronting demons and expelling them. It is this action that we are directed to follow in our warfare. When the disciples went out as the representatives of Jesus, exercising His authority, they discovered to their intense joy that demons had to obey them. As followers of Jesus, we walk in that same authority.

Please grasp fully the words of Jesus: "Behold, I give you the authority to trample on serpents and scorpions, and over all the power of the enemy."

When we become representatives of God's Kingdom, then God, through Jesus, gives us authority to trample on the representatives of Satan's kingdom that are afflicting us, and to overcome all the power of the enemy. The total victory and authority of Jesus is now vested in us as the representatives of His Kingdom.

Then, lest we should be afraid, Jesus closes with, *"Nothing will harm you."* Jesus did not give that promise for the benefit of those disciples alone. It is a pattern for each subsequent generation of believers who would follow. In our generation, you and I go forth in the name of Jesus to administer Jesus' victory and authority over all the representatives of Satan's kingdom. Like the disciples, nothing will harm us. The victory of the cross has prepared us as His people ultimately to be the instruments of overcoming evil in these end times.

4

A New Creation

Once we understand that Satan is a defeated foe, we can engage in warfare with confidence as Jesus' Kingdom representatives. While the deceiver will try to keep us from recognizing this truth, Scripture reveals that Jesus has already prepared the way for us to administer His authority. Through His incarnation, Jesus became the "last Adam" (see 1 Corinthians 15:45). He took upon Himself all the guilt, condemnation and curse of the Adamic race, and sealed it off by His death and burial. Next, He rose again from the dead on the third day to become the "second Man" (verse 47). As such He is the head of a new race that is to be the instrument of overcoming evil in this age.

Who are the members of this new race? All who are united with Christ by faith in His death, burial and resurrection, and who are regenerated (or born again). We are His Body, the Church, and He is the head.

Parallels between the Two Races

God's desire for this new race is to fulfill the purposes that Adam failed to fulfill. Let's look briefly at the parallels between the first Adam and his race and the last Adam, Jesus, and the new race that comes forth from Him.

To begin with, Adam was created with the inbreathed breath of God (see Genesis 2:7). The new race is brought into being as each person is regenerated individually by the inbreathed Spirit from the Lord Jesus Christ (see John 20:19–22).

Second, the first Adam was created in God's likeness and image. In the new race, the image of God is being restored through the work of the Holy Spirit, bringing forth the likeness of the Lord Jesus Christ in us (see Colossians 3:10).

Third, God's purpose for the first Adam was to exercise God-given dominion or authority over all the earth. Likewise for the new race, God's purpose is that we should be His ambassadors—heaven's official representatives, carrying heaven's message and exercising heavenly authority. To accomplish this, God has placed all the authority of heaven's government behind us. Jesus says to the new race, "All authority is given to Me. Go, therefore, and exercise it" (see Matthew 28:18–20).

Fourth, the first Adam was brought into being to have intelligent partnership with God. He was not a slave; he was in fellowship. He shared the outworking and fulfillment of God's purposes in creation. Likewise, to the new race Jesus says, "I don't call you slaves any longer, I call you friends" (see John 15:15). Paul says we are co-workers with God (see 1 Corinthians 3:9; 2 Corinthians 6:1) and stewards of God's household (see 1 Corinthians 4:1; 1 Peter 4:10).

Fifth, in the first creation the provision of a mate for Adam was unique because Eve was brought into being out of Adam.

This corresponds to the provision of the Church as a Bride for the Lord Jesus Christ. As Adam slept, Eve was brought forth out of his body. As Jesus slept in the tomb, the Church was brought forth out of His sacrificial, substitutionary death. As Eve was presented to Adam, so the Church will be presented to Christ (see Ephesians 5:25–27, 31–32).

Our purpose as the new race is summed up by Jesus' words to His disciples: "As the Father has sent Me, I also send you" (John 20:21). We are here on earth to fulfill the same relationship toward Christ as Christ fulfilled on the earth toward His Father. Christ lived in union with the Father; we live in union with Christ. Christ lived to do the Father's will; we live to do the will of Christ. The words and works of Christ came from the Father; the words and works of the believer come from Christ. Christ revealed the Father to the world; the believer reveals Christ to the world. The parallel is absolutely exact.

Reversing the Result

We understand, then, that we are a new race—Kingdom representatives with a purpose to fulfill. Knowing that Jesus sends us forth in the same way the Father sent Him, we find our directive in 1 John 3:8: "For this purpose the Son of God was manifested, that He might destroy the works of the devil."

This tells us one primary reason that Jesus was manifested in human flesh: *to destroy the works of the devil.* The word that is translated *destroy* here (Greek, *lysē*) means literally "to loose" or "to undo." The same word is used when John the Baptist said concerning the Messiah, "I am not worthy to stoop down and undo his shoelaces" (see Luke 3:16).

The works of the devil that Jesus came to undo relate to five specific results of Adam's disastrous fall in the Garden of Eden. It is our challenge as a new race to take our places of authority in Jesus' Kingdom and reverse those results. In the remainder of this chapter and the four chapters following, we will explore the ways in which we do so.

First Reversal: A Change in Nature

When Adam disobeyed God and fell into sin, there was a change in his nature. The key word to describe the change is *corruption*. Adam, and through him the entire race, became corrupt both spiritually and physically.

As a result of Christ's death and resurrection, however, a new nature is brought into being in the believer that reverses or undoes the corruption produced by the Fall. In Colossians 3:10, Paul writes, "Put on the new man who is renewed in knowledge according to the image of Him who created him."

For a better translation for the phrase *is renewed* I would suggest *is being renewed*. The verb is a continuous present, meaning that it is an ongoing process. The word *knowledge* also means "acknowledging" in the sense of reproducing His image. Each of us individually is being renewed or brought back.

This renewal is the first way that the new race in Christ reverses the results of Adam's fall and deals a blow to the enemy. A new nature is brought into being in the believer that undoes the corruption. Believers are being brought back into the knowledge of—and into the acknowledging of—the Creator in such a way that we become a new creation.

Made in His Image

Here is a beautiful thought. In the first creation, God did not rest until He had produced His own image and likeness.

He rested the seventh day because on the sixth day He had brought forth a creation who was a reproduction of His own image—the man Adam. In the new creation, God will not rest until He has reproduced His own image and likeness in the believer. This is more fully stated in 2 Peter 1:2–4. This passage is one long sentence containing several powerful words. Included in these verses is one of the most astonishing statements made anywhere in Scripture.

> Grace and peace be multiplied to you in the knowledge of God and of Jesus our Lord, as His divine power has given to us all things that pertain to life and godliness, through the knowledge of Him who called us by glory and virtue, by which have been given to us exceedingly great and precious promises, that through these you may be partakers of the divine nature, having escaped the corruption that is in the world through lust.

Notice at the beginning of this passage, everything is coming through the knowledge, or acknowledging, of God and Jesus.

Everything Is Already Provided

In this profound passage of Scripture, we are able to trace certain successive statements in Peter's thought. Beginning at the first part of verse 3, we see that God's divine power *has given* to us—not will give, but *has given*—all things that pertain to life and godliness. In the new creation, every provision has already been made—just as it was in the old creation. When God brought Adam into the world, He did not look around for a place to put him, nor did He search for nourishing items with which to feed him. Adam was brought into a perfect creation where every need had been foreseen and already met.

The preparation and provision is exactly the same in the new creation in Christ. When we are created anew in Christ, we are placed into a provision that is already complete and perfect. There were no afterthoughts. God did not have to add anything. All the provision we will ever need for time and eternity has already been made ready for us in Christ. This provision includes spiritual life, physical life, life in this world and life in the world to come.

Many people pray ineffective prayers that cannot be answered—because they are asking God to give them something that He *has already given them*. My personal belief is that most times God does not grant answers to that type of prayer because to do so would create misunderstanding in us. Many times I hear Christians pleading for something that they want God to give them. If He were to speak to them, He might have to say, "I gave it to you long ago; it's already yours in Christ Jesus."

Go and Possess

Notice in this Scripture that everything has been given to us "through the knowledge of Him who called us by glory and virtue." Everything God has for us is always contained in the knowledge of Jesus Christ. In verse 4, we read that the provision is made available to us by "exceedingly great and precious promises." If we will study God's Word and lay hold of the promises, everything we could possibly need is contained there.

In my years of teaching I have often made the following comparison: Under the Old Covenant under a leader named Joshua, God brought His people into a Promised Land. Under the New Covenant under a leader named Jesus (in Hebrew it is the same as Joshua), God brings His people into a land of promises. What is the difference? In the Old Testament, a Promised Land; in the New Testament, a land of promises. God said about the land He had promised to Israel, "It's a good land. Everything you'll ever need is there. It's a land flowing with milk and honey. The water it drinks is the rain of heaven. You don't need to work for it—digging the wells, or planting the vineyards or the olive groves. All you must do is go in and possess it."

In Christ, it is exactly the same. God says, "I don't have to do any more. It's all there in the promises. Go in and possess them."

The Divine Nature

The result of possessing the promises is stated in verse 4 of the above Scripture: "Through these [promises] you may be partakers of the divine nature." *Divine nature* means we have become partakers of the nature of God Himself. What is the result? We have "escaped the corruption that is in the world through lust."

Please notice that key word again: *corruption*. Adam's fall brought spiritual and physical corruption. Christ's redemption delivers us from that corruption and makes us partakers of the very nature of God Himself. This takes place in us through the provision of God. That provision is in the knowledge of Jesus Christ, which we appropriate by finding and applying the promises of the Word of God to our lives.

We can summarize this amazing process in one statement: *Christ, being divine, became also human, that the believer, being human, might become also divine.* Jesus, who was divine, became human. He did not cease to be divine, but He became human—that the believer, being human, might become also divine without ceasing to be human.

The divine nature comes to us through the promises of the Word of God—because the Word of God is an incorruptible seed: "Having been born again, not of corruptible seed but incorruptible, through the word of God which lives and abides forever" (1 Peter 1:23). As we appropriate the incorruptible seed of God's Word into our lives, it reproduces an incorruptible nature in us. We become a new creation. As that takes place, we succeed in the first reversal of the effects of the Fall: We become partakers of the divine nature and escape the corruption that is in the world.

Let's look now at the second result that came upon the human race and all of creation as a result of the fall of Adam and how, through Jesus Christ, we reverse it.

5

Authority Reinstated

In our previous chapter we introduced a basic premise. We saw that one of the reasons for taking our place with Jesus Christ as a new race is to reverse the effects of Adam's fall. We discovered that the first of these reversals is accomplished as we become a new creation with a divine nature.

In this chapter, we explore the second reversal: renewed authority. The second result of the Fall was that Satan usurped the realm of authority that God had given to Adam. Before Jesus' crucifixion, He referred to Satan as "the ruler of this world" (John 12:31; 14:30; 16:11). Also, in the temptation in the wilderness, Satan showed Jesus all the kingdoms of the world in a moment of time and said, "All this authority I will give you." Why was Satan able to say that? Because at that point, it was Satan's to give.

The death and resurrection of Jesus Christ changed all that: Authority was taken from Satan and reinvested in the Lord Jesus Christ. Because Christ had removed the guilt of the Adamic race, it was now possible for God to make this authority available to the new race without compromising

His righteousness. This is one of the great revelations of the New Testament. Because of the death and resurrection of Jesus, He, the last Adam, could say, "All authority in heaven and in earth is now given unto Me." Consequently, He can say to us, "Go, therefore . . ." In other words, Jesus is saying to us: "You are now the ones to administer My authority. I have obtained the authority, but I'm going back to heaven. It is to be exercised by you who believe in Me and who are now My representatives on earth."

The Exaltation of Jesus

Paul elaborates on this transfer of authority to Jesus and to us.

> [God] worked [His mighty power] in Christ when He raised Him from the dead and seated Him at His right hand in the heavenly places, far above all principality and power and might and dominion, and every name that is named, not only in this age but also in that which is to come. And He put all things under His feet, and gave Him to be head over all things to the church, which is His body, the fullness of Him who fills all in all.
>
> Ephesians 1:20–23

Similar references to the exaltation of Jesus are made in Philippians 2:9–11, and 1 Peter 3:22. Here is the point: Jesus has been exalted far above all realms of authority in the created universe. He is the head, exalted at the Father's right hand, far above all principality, power, might and dominion.

That being true, let's see where you and I, as believers in Christ, fit into this picture of exaltation. Ephesians 2:5–6 explains that we are identified with Christ in every phase of His exaltation—right up to His position on the throne: "Even when we were dead in trespasses, [God] made us alive together with Christ (by grace you have been saved), and raised us up together, and made us sit together in the heavenly places in Christ Jesus."

Our identification with Christ does not cease when we are made alive and brought forth out of the tomb. It goes right on to the throne. I compare this to getting into an elevator, which is Jesus Christ. When you first press button "B," you go down to the basement—for burial and baptism. After that, you can press any button on the panel. Whatever button you press will determine the height to which you will go. God has made it possible for you to go to the penthouse if you like, because in Christ we have been raised up from the burial of the tomb and made to sit together with Him on His throne.

A fellow minister once pointed out a great truth from this passage—one that has gripped me ever since I first heard it. My friend said, "Notice that God has guarded the access to the throne. The access is not a wide-open door: It is crucifixion, burial and resurrection. Those who are not willing to be crucified with Christ and buried with Christ have no right of access to the throne."

How true! The old man—the old Adamic nature—has no place on the throne. The universe would disintegrate within five minutes if the old Adam ever got there. Only through the process of crucifixion, burial and resurrection is one eligible to step into the elevator and press the button for the penthouse.

Reigning in Life

Our next question concerns the timeframe of this exaltation in Christ and sharing of His authority. Romans 5:17 gives us the answer: "For if by the one man's offense [Adam's sin] death reigned through the one, much more those who receive abundance of grace and of the gift of righteousness will reign in life through the One, Jesus Christ."

Because of Adam's offense, death reigned over the whole human race. Death was a despot—a king ruling with unchallenged dominion.

And yet, this passage tells us that we now reign in life through Christ. This is not referring to some future age. It is *in life*, right now! We should be on the throne reigning in life with Jesus Christ.

Notice also the contrast described here between Satan and Jesus. Satan is a despot. Under his dominion, there is only one will—Satan's. When Jesus came to undo the works of Satan, however, He made it possible for us to escape the dominion of darkness and to be exalted together with Him. Contrast also the nature of Satan and the nature of God. Satan will not share anything with anybody. God longs to share everything with everyone who believes and meets the conditions. He invites us now to share the throne with Him and to reign with Him as kings in life.

A Kingdom of Priests

A further thought about our position appears in the salutation of the apostle John to the seven churches: "To Him who loved us and washed us from our sins in His own blood, and has made us kings and priests to His God and Father" (Revelation 1:5–6).

Other translations of these verses read "a kingdom of priests," but that does not matter for our purposes. The point is that we have two functions in Christ: to reign as kings and to minister as priests. Both functions are fulfilled through one element—the blood of Jesus.

I was once talking to a man who said, "In my church, it takes nine years to become a priest."

I said, "Isn't it wonderful that a believer becomes a priest through the blood of Jesus in one moment?"

Through the blood of Jesus, we have been made both kings and priests: kings to rule and priests to offer spiritual sacrifice and to intercede. I believe these are the three supreme ministries of the believer in Christ: ruling, offering sacrifice and interceding. In Revelation 5:9–10 we find this same thought expressed in a song of praise to Christ:

> "You are worthy to take the scroll, and to open its seals; for You were slain, and have redeemed us to God by Your blood out of every tribe and tongue and people and nation, and have made us kings and priests to our God; and we shall reign on the earth."

Once again, we are called "kings and priests." Even when Peter uses the term "a royal priesthood" (1 Peter 2:9), the combination is still the same.

This is very interesting because the combination refers to the fact that Jesus is a High Priest after the order of Melchizedek (Hebrews 6:19–8:6). This is actually the original priesthood. Melchizedek is introduced in Genesis 14:18 as "king of Salem" and "the priest of God Most High." *Melchizedek* in Hebrew means "the king of righteousness" (Hebrews 7:2). He was also the king of Salem, which means "king of peace." In Melchizedek these two great offices are combined.

Under the Law of Moses, priesthood and kingship were separated. The kingship went to the tribe of Judah and the priesthood went to the tribe of Levi. In Christ, however, as High Priest after the order of Melchizedek, kingship and priesthood are restored in the one person.

The significance for us is this: We are in the same position through Christ. We are kings and priests. David was a king under the Law, but he could not be a priest. Aaron was a priest, but could not be a king. In Christ, we can be both.

Three Realms

Let's turn to one other Scripture that reveals the completeness of Christ's dominion. In Revelation 1:18, Jesus is speaking: "I am He who lives, and was dead, and behold, I am alive forevermore. Amen. And I have the keys of Hades and of Death." Jesus holds the keys to all three realms: (1) heaven, (2) earth (see Matthew 28:18), and (3) the lower realm of Hades and Death. That same authority has now been given to the believer to exercise on His behalf.

Adam was created in the visible likeness of God, and God gave him dominion over all the earth. He was God's visible, personal, authorized representative, exercising God's authority on His behalf to the entirety of creation over which he was placed in charge.

Likewise, we in Christ are God's visible, personal, authorized representatives, exercising Christ's authority on His behalf. But our place of authority is not limited to the earth where Adam had dominion. A great hymn states, "The blessings that were lost in Adam are more than restored in Christ." This is so true! We do not just get back the earthly dominion. Rather, in Christ we are given a spiritual dominion that covers all three realms: heaven, earth and the lower realm as well.

In our next chapter we will discuss the third way that we reverse the results of Adam's fall: spiritual dominion over the demons harassing us here on earth. In later chapters we will discuss how, through our victory in Jesus, we will be the instruments to cast down Satan's kingdom from the heavenlies.

6

Authority Over Demons

In our previous two chapters, we have seen how the redeemed work of Jesus Christ has undone the work of Satan in two significant ways. First, it has secured our standing as a new creation in the image of God. Next, it has situated us here on earth as Christ's visible, authorized representatives.

In this chapter, we will discuss the reversal from the third result of Adam's fall—the human race becoming subject to demonic harassment and control. We reverse this, however, since in Christ, believers are now given authority over the demons. Part of our salvation in Christ is being delivered personally from the fear and oppression of evil spirits, and then being given authority over them.

Luke 1 records the prophecy of the father of John the Baptist, Zacharias, which is a kind of introduction to the Gospel dispensation of which John was to be the forerunner. Speaking about what is to come through the Messiah, as the fulfillment of God's promises under the Old Covenant, Zacharias said, "[God] spoke by the mouth of His

43

holy prophets . . . that we should be saved from our enemies and from the hand of all who hate us" (Luke 1:70–71).

In Christ we experience this truth. We are "saved from our enemies and from the hand of all who hate us." Our overall enemy, Satan, and his angels are in the heavenlies. But our enemy at hand—the evil spirits that are personally present to harass and torment us—are the demons.

Living without Fear

Luke gives us further insight regarding how we are to operate in this realm to overcome evil: "To grant us that we, being delivered from the hand of our enemies, might serve Him without fear, in holiness and righteousness before Him all the days of our life" (Luke 1:74–75).

Here is the resounding truth of these verses: You cannot serve God in holiness and righteousness all the days of your life until you have been delivered out of the hand of your enemies. Deliverance from evil is essential to full service, and the enemies of whom the Scripture speaks here primarily are the evil spirits.

A person who is not fully delivered cannot serve without fear. This is true of multitudes of sincere Christians who are serving—but not without fear. Why? Because they have not been fully delivered from the torment and harassment of evil spirits. God has provided deliverance to serve Him without fear in holiness and righteousness for our entire lives. This is not speaking of the next world. This is for us in this world—in this life now. We can have full deliverance from the harassment and oppression of all demon spirits.

I find very, very few Christians who serve without fear. The majority of Christians worry about what evil may befall them—some in the spiritual realm of accusation and torment, some in the physical realm of sickness, and some in the financial realm of poverty or frustration.

Personally, I find that almost every morning when I wake up, fear is waiting at the door to get in. If I do not immediately establish my place in Christ and begin to thank and praise God for who and what I am in Christ, I will not spend that day in complete liberty. A sort of nagging, tormenting fear will assail my mind. When I look at myself in the mirror as I am shaving I say, "Thank You, Jesus. You took my infirmities. You bore my sicknesses, and with Your stripes I am healed."

By the time I have said that three times, I am believing it. Every day, I must reestablish myself in my place in Christ. I do not know if this is true for everyone, but I think the way you begin the first five minutes of the day is usually decisive as to how you will spend the rest of the day. I am not talking about spending hours in prayer; it is simply reminding yourself who you are and where you are in Christ. You remind yourself of what Christ has done to the devil and the fact that the devil has no right of access to you. You and I can serve Jesus without fear, having been delivered from the hands of our enemies.

Dealing with Demons

As a result of Christ's work, not only do we not need to fear the demons, but here is the other side of the coin: *The demons need to fear us*. Believe me, they do. They try to keep this fact from us—and their main weapon is bluff. I have many times encountered a demon that would roar like a lion, shout and use blasphemy. When the authority of Christ was pressed against it, however, it began to whimper and sob like a naughty child.

Clearly, Jesus has given us authority over demonic spirits. Matthew 10:1 confirms this fact: "And when He had called His twelve disciples to Him, He gave them power [Greek, authority] over unclean spirits, to cast them out, and to heal all kinds of sickness and all kinds of disease."

The two words *kinds of* were put in by the translators. It is not necessarily a mistranslation, but the text actually reads "all sickness and all disease." That rendering helps us understand exactly the authority we have been given in Christ.

At one point in His ministry Jesus sent out seventy disciples before Him to prepare the way. When they returned, they announced the amazing discovery they had made. "Then the seventy returned with joy, saying, 'Lord, even the demons are subject to us in Your name'" (Luke 10:17).

What a thrilling discovery for men who had witnessed the effects of demonic oppression all their lives! "When we cast out demons in the name of Jesus, they get out!"

I remember one occasion when I was preaching about deliverance. Near the end of my sermon in a packed church, a woman stood up and started to scream abuse at me. Of course, it was not the woman—it was a demon. I stopped and said, "Satan, you've challenged me publicly. I'm a servant of Jesus Christ, and you've got to be humbled publicly." Then I said, "In the name of Jesus, I command you to bow before me."

I do not think I would always do that, but I felt a leading from the Holy Spirit to do so on this occasion. It took about three or four minutes, but the woman fell to her knees right there in the pew with the astonished congregation looking on. It so happened she was a deacon's wife!

Afterward, when my wife was praying with her, she said, "You know, I knew I had an evil spirit. But every time I went for help they said, 'You're a Christian; you couldn't have an evil spirit.'"

She knew, however, that she was right, and that night she was delivered from a spirit of depression.

The next day she told us, "I went to bed that night knowing I was free." Then she added, "Brother Prince, you may not believe me, but that spirit came and sat on the quilt and said, 'I'm coming back.' But I said, 'No, you won't.' And it left!"

This incident illustrates just how real this conflict is.

Look at the words of Jesus to the seventy who returned: "Behold, I give you the authority . . . over all the power of the enemy, and nothing shall by any means hurt you" (Luke 10:19). How many Christians believe that? No flu bug, no virus—nothing shall by any means hurt you.

I believe we are entitled to rejoice when we see captive humanity set free. It is a legitimate cause of joy. Clearly this authority over "all the power of the enemy" represents an area lost in the Fall that we reverse in the name of Jesus.

7

Freedom from Futility

In the last few chapters, we have examined three significant areas where the new race in Christ—the redeemed race who are called to defeat the enemy in this present age—is to reverse the effects of Adam's fall. Those areas are: (1) living as new creations, bearing the image of Jesus Christ; (2) demonstrating the authority Jesus has given us; and (3) exercising that authority over the evil spirits that confront us. In this chapter, we will examine the fourth area of our release from the Fall: freedom from futility.

As a result of the Fall, the whole of Adam's area of dominion was made subject to futility. *Futility* may be defined as "ultimate failure and frustration." This is part of our responsibility as the new race in Christ: to be the instrument of redemption from futility for all of creation.

Scripture explains this as part of the total, logical unfolding plan of redemption.

> For the earnest expectation of the creation eagerly waits for the revealing of the sons of God. For the creation was

subjected to futility, not willingly, but because of Him who subjected it in hope; because the creation itself also will be delivered from the bondage of corruption into the glorious liberty of the children of God. For we know that the whole creation groans and labors with birth pangs together until now. Not only that, but we also who have the firstfruits of the Spirit, even we ourselves groan within ourselves, eagerly waiting for the adoption, the redemption of our body.

Romans 8:19–23

The futility and corruption will continue until the children of God are resurrected and manifested in their glory. All of creation is waiting for this event to occur. For now, however, all creation suffers, as if in the throes of the birth of that new age.

Every believer who is born again through faith in Christ is given authority to become a child of God (see John 1:12). Only when our bodies are completely and finally redeemed at the resurrection by the transformation into the likeness of Jesus' resurrection body will redemption come to the creation.

Futility came to the creation through the fall of the Adamic race; redemption will come to the creation through the restoration of the Adamic race. God's program is absolutely perfect in every detail.

Colossians 3:3–4 adds a helpful insight to this premise of redemption coming through us as new creations: "For you died, and your life is hidden with Christ in God. When Christ who is our life appears, then you also will appear with Him in glory."

You have an invisible life that is not evident to the senses. The world cannot see it; you have it hidden with Christ in God. To me, one of the most thrilling statements in all of

Scripture is *Christ who is our life*. As of this moment, this life, which is hidden with Christ in God, remains in the heavenlies where it cannot be seen. But when Christ who is our life shall appear or be revealed, then we shall also appear with Him in glory.

This revealing of the glory of the children of God is the same glory that Paul refers to in Romans 8:21. When Jesus, the Son of God, is revealed in His glory, then we shall be revealed in glory together with Him, sharing His physical likeness. At that moment, the revelation of the glory of the children of God at the resurrection will bring redemption to the creation.

The Millennium

This redemption, as I understand it, will come in two successive phases. First, there is a period of a thousand years called the *Millennium*—when Christ will reign on earth with Jerusalem as the center of His Kingdom. During this period the reversal of futility will be partial. Then, beyond the Millennium, there will be a further period of God's dealings when the redemption will be perfect.

The prophet Isaiah gives us a picture of Christ's millennial Kingdom.

> With righteousness He shall judge the poor, and decide with equity for the meek of the earth; He shall strike the earth with the rod of His mouth, and with the breath of His lips He shall slay the wicked. Righteousness shall be the belt of His loins, and faithfulness the belt of His waist. "The wolf also shall dwell with the lamb, the leopard shall lie down with the young goat, the calf and the young lion and the fatling together; and a little child shall lead them. The cow and the

bear shall graze; their young ones shall lie down together; and the lion shall eat straw like the ox."

Isaiah 11:4–7

When He smites the earth "with the rod of His mouth," this will be His coming in judgment on behalf of the meek, the downtrodden and the oppressed. I believe the wicked one being slain here is the Antichrist, because Scripture reveals that the Antichrist will be consumed by the breath that comes from the lips of the Christ (see 2 Thessalonians 2:8).

Part of the futility in creation is the cruelty and savagery we see in the animal kingdom, which is a result of the Fall. It was not this way at the beginning. In the original creation, no animal ate or preyed upon another creature. My understanding is that hostility in the animal kingdom was the result of the release of the demonic hordes that came when Adam's kingdom was turned over to Satan.

It is demonic influence that makes the lion fierce and the cat cruel. I was told of a man who was a missionary in Africa who was being mauled by a lion. As he was just about to be torn to pieces, all he could say was, "Jesus!" When he said this, the lion turned and fled. The lion apparently recognized the authority in the name of Jesus.

Somebody once said, "Nature arrayed in fang and claw." But that was not always the case; it is part of futility. When futility is finally revoked, the lion shall eat straw like the ox. This picture of tranquility is also portrayed in Isaiah 11:8–9:

> The nursing child shall play by the cobra's hole, and the weaned child shall put his hand in the viper's den. They shall not hurt nor destroy in all My holy mountain, for the earth shall be full of the knowledge of the LORD as the waters cover the sea.

This situation takes place in the Millennium when God's grace revokes the curse. If you stop to consider, in Noah's ark there must have been a remarkable dispensation of God's grace for Noah to keep all those animals together for several months without a conflict. Every animal that stepped into the ark underwent a change of nature, even if it was only temporary.

Noah's ark is a picture of being in Christ. When we step into Christ we stop hating one another, we stop despising other races, and we begin to love one another. If you have not had that change of nature, I question whether you ever got into the ark.

Isaiah gives us another picture of the Millennium.

> "For behold, I create new heavens and a new earth; and the former shall not be remembered or come to mind. But be glad and rejoice forever in what I create; for behold, I create Jerusalem as a rejoicing, and her people a joy. I will rejoice in Jerusalem, and joy in My people; the voice of weeping shall no longer be heard in her, nor the voice of crying. No more shall an infant from there live but a few days, nor an old man who has not fulfilled his days; for the child shall die one hundred years old, but the sinner being one hundred years old shall be accursed."
>
> Isaiah 65:17–20

During this time there will no premature death; everyone will live out the full span of years. There will still be sinners, but even they will be affected by the grace of God. Even so, this is not complete and final redemption.

The Fullness of Times

If we look on beyond the Millennium to what is called "the dispensation of the fullness of times" or "the completion" or "fulfilling of God's purposes for the ages," we see the complete work of redemption from futility and corruption. Paul writes concerning this complete work: "Having made known to us the mystery of His will, according to His good pleasure which He purposed in Himself, that in the dispensation of the fullness of the times He might gather together in one all things in Christ" (Ephesians 1:9–10).

The "fullness of times" to which Paul refers is the dispensation beyond the Millennium—the consummation of God's purposes for all ages. This same principle is also referred to in 1 Corinthians 15:28, when Christ shall offer up the Kingdom to the Father "that God may be all in all." We have a special place in that dispensation because we first trusted in Christ. Throughout all ages, therefore, we shall be to the praise of the glory of His grace.

The apostle John presents us with one of the most complete pictures of this final result of redemption from futility.

> Now I saw a new heaven and a new earth, for the first heaven and the first earth had passed away. Also there was no more sea. Then I, John, saw the holy city, New Jerusalem, coming down out of heaven from God, prepared as a bride adorned for her husband. And I heard a loud voice from heaven saying, "Behold, the tabernacle of God is with men, and He will dwell with them, and they shall be His people. God Himself will be with them and be their God. And God will wipe away every tear from their eyes; there shall be no more death, nor sorrow, nor crying. There shall be no more pain, for the former things have passed away."
>
> Revelation 21:1–4

This is a picture of total redemption from futility in every form: travail, sorrow, birth pain, sickness, disease. They are all wiped out. The description continues.

Then one of the seven angels who had the seven bowls filled with the seven last plagues came to me and talked with me, saying, "Come, I will show you the bride, the Lamb's wife."

Verse 9

What the angel showed John was the New Jerusalem. Remember, the New Jerusalem is not heaven. It is the final manifestation of the Church in which God will indwell creation. This is His supreme purpose—to create in us a dwelling place in which He can thereafter make Himself available to all creation. The result is revealed in these verses:

And the nations of those who are saved shall walk in its light, and the kings of the earth bring their glory and honor into it. Its gates shall not be shut at all by day (there shall be no night there). And they shall bring the glory and the honor of the nations into it.

Verses 24–26

As the redeemed people of God, we shall be the center of the universe. How will that take place? Because God will be dwelling in us and we will be the place to which all the nations that are then in the world will bring their worship and honor. At that point, vanity will be eliminated. Every curse, pain and sickness will be eliminated. All enmity, strife, separation and bitterness will be done away with. There will be nothing to divide and nothing to make bitter.

Futility will be eliminated. This reversal will all be centered in the new creation in Christ, the Bride of the Lamb. Just as futility came through the first Adam, through the new race under the second Man, Jesus Christ, futility will be abolished.

8

Overcoming Satan's Kingdom

In previous chapters, we have covered four of the five areas in which Christ's redemptive work has reversed the effects of Adam's fall. In this chapter, we will look at the fifth area in which the Church is to defeat the enemy by demonstrating the victory won at the cross.

The final consequence of Adam's fall was that the Adamic race became identified with Satan in his guilt and therefore subject to the judgment of God. Through Christ's death and resurrection, the new race became identified with Christ in His righteousness. This means that we have dominion over Satan, over all his kingdom and over all his forces. We now have become the instruments God will use to cast down Satan's kingdom. This is the great truth that I believe Satan seeks to keep from believers.

More Than Conquerors

Let's begin with Romans 5:1: "Therefore, having been justified by faith, we have peace with God through our Lord Jesus

Christ." We are justified, made righteous. My definition of *justified* is "just-as-if-I'd" never sinned. Furthermore, Paul says, "There is therefore now no condemnation to those who are in Christ Jesus" (Romans 8:1). If we are in that place where there is no condemnation, then we are in a place where we are undefeatable. Paul extends this further:

> Who shall bring a charge against God's elect? It is God who justifies. Who is he who condemns? It is Christ who died, and furthermore is also risen, who is even at the right hand of God, who also makes intercession for us. Who shall separate us from the love of Christ?
>
> Verses 33–35

Notice these three questions: Who shall lay anything to our charge? Who shall condemn? Who shall separate? Every one of these questions is answered in Jesus Christ.

> As it is written: "For Your sake we are killed all day long; we are accounted as sheep for the slaughter." Yet in all these things we are more than conquerors through Him who loved us. For I am persuaded that neither death nor life, nor angels nor principalities nor powers, nor things present nor things to come, nor height nor depth, nor any other created thing, shall be able to separate us from the love of God which is in Christ Jesus our Lord.
>
> Verses 36–39

Please take note of this amazing truth: Neither angels, principalities nor powers have any dominion over us now. Why? Because in Christ we have been exalted "far above all principality and power and might and dominion, and every name that is named, not only in this age but also in that which is to come" (Ephesians 1:21). The basis of this entire victorious state for us is recognizing our righteousness in Christ. Paul states, "For He made Him who knew no sin to be sin for us, that we might become the righteousness of God in Him" (2 Corinthians 5:21).

We are no longer guilty or subject to condemnation because we have been made righteous—justified, just-as-if-I'd never sinned. Because of Christ's righteousness, we now have authority over the kingdom of Satan, and we become the instruments by which Satan's kingdom will be cast down.

Total Transformation

Other Scriptures reinforce our authority and position in Christ. It is important that this truth becomes deeply implanted in our hearts. Look at Colossians 1:13: "[God] hath delivered us from the power [authority] of darkness, and hath translated us into the kingdom of his dear Son" (KJV).

I am using the King James Version for this verse because the translation is more vivid. *Translate* means "to carry across totally—spirit, soul and body." Two men in the Old Testament were translated: Enoch and Elijah. Both of them went completely into God's presence. In the same way, you and I have been translated out of the authority of darkness into the Kingdom of the Son of God's love—spirit, soul and body. We are no longer under Satan's authority; we are in the Kingdom of God in Christ. *Satan has no rights over us and no claims against us.*

Paul prayed for the Christians that they might "spirit, soul, and body be preserved blameless at the coming of our Lord Jesus Christ" (1 Thessalonians 5:23). This action by God is a translation. It is not a partial transfer in which a portion of our being is left under the authority of Satan. We have been totally moved over from one realm to the other realm.

Look next at 2 Corinthians 10:4–5: "For the weapons of our warfare are not carnal but mighty in God for pulling down strongholds."

In this spiritual warfare to which we are called in Christ, we have the weapons that will cast down Satan's stronghold and every high thing that exalts itself against the knowledge of God. Please take a moment to meditate on the meaning of that phrase *every high thing that exalts itself against the knowledge of God*. This includes the entire kingdom of Satan. This passage makes it clear that God has provided us with the weapons to cast that kingdom down.

The Last Great Conflict

Jesus said, "On this rock I will build My church, and the gates of Hades shall not prevail against it" (Matthew 16:18). Let me mention first what this verse does *not* mean. The Church is not being besieged in a city in which the devil is unable to batter the gates down. Rather, here is what this passage signifies: The Church will attack the gates of Hades, and the gates of Hades will not be able to keep the Church out, because Jesus has the keys of Death and of Hades (see Revelation 1:18).

We see this truth affirmed as well in Romans 16:20. There Paul tells the believers in Rome that "the God of peace will crush Satan under your feet shortly." As the Church takes her stand on the authority Christ has given us, Satan will very soon be bruised under the feet of the believer.

Revelation depicts the last great conflict of this age in which Satan and his angels will be cast out of heaven: "And they overcame him by the blood of the Lamb and by the word of their testimony, and they did not love their lives to the death" (Revelation 12:11).

In other words, it is the believers on earth who are to win the victory over Satan. Our victory will cause him to be cast down out of his rival, rebellious kingdom in the heavenlies— a truth we will discuss in detail in the very last chapter of this book.

Here is my belief: The devil wants to keep us in the dark. If there is one truth that the devil wants to keep us from knowing, it is that we have the authority to bring his kingdom to an end. Until we know it, we will not do it. But when we know it, we must determine to do it.

How God plans to prepare His Church for the coming conflict is the subject of the next chapter.

9

God's Program for the Close of the Age

We have considered five ways in which the new race of believers in Christ is to reverse the results of Adam's fall. First, the change that occurred in Adam's nature is to be reversed as believers are to become partakers of the divine nature, escaping the corruption that is in the world.

Second, the authority that Satan usurped from Adam has now been restored to Christ. Through Jesus Christ, this authority is transferred to the new race, which is the Church. That authority is now to be exercised by the new race on Christ's behalf.

Third, believers have been delivered from the harassment and control of evil spirits. In fact, they have been given authority over evil spirits, the outworking of which is to be exercised in the name of Jesus.

Fourth, the condition of vanity and futility that came to creation through Adam's fall will be removed. In the restoration that ensues, creation will be delivered from futility through what the Bible calls "the manifestation of the glory of the sons of God." This manifestation is associated with the resurrection of believers—including all of God's purposes and dispensations that follow resurrection.

Fifth, through Adam's fall, the Adamic race became identified with Satan in his guilt and in his rebellion. Through Christ's redemption, believers have become identified with Christ in His righteousness and thus commissioned to be the instruments to cast down Satan's kingdom.

A Work of Restoration

As we anticipate the conflict of overcoming evil in these end times, we need to understand how God intends to help us. Many passages of Scripture foretell that at the close of this present evil age, there will be a special intervention of God in sovereign grace on behalf of His people. This intervention will not be something that we have earned or that comes because we deserve it; it is simply a provision of God's grace to fulfill this mission with which we have been charged as the new race.

On the Day of Pentecost, immediately after the outpouring of the Holy Spirit and the first public manifestation of the Church of Jesus Christ in its new power and authority, here is what occurred. The apostle Peter proclaimed God's purpose for the close of the age. Quoting from the prophet Joel, he declared:

> But this is what was spoken by the prophet Joel: "And it shall come to pass in the last days, says God, that I will pour out of My Spirit on all flesh; your sons and your daughters shall prophesy, your young men shall see visions, your old men shall dream dreams. And on My menservants and on My

maidservants I will pour out My Spirit in those days; and they shall prophesy. I will show wonders in heaven above and signs in the earth beneath: blood and fire and vapor of smoke. The sun shall be turned into darkness, and the moon into blood, before the coming of the great and awesome day of the LORD. And it shall come to pass that whoever calls on the name of the LORD shall be saved."

Acts 2:16–21

This passage is a proclamation by almighty God as to what He will do. Many of the promises of God's Word are conditional; in other words, we must do something in order for God to fulfill His promise. Their fulfillment depends upon the believer meeting a certain condition. This promise, however, is an unconditional promise. There are no prior conditions attached.

God says, "In the last days I will pour out of My Spirit upon all flesh." He does not say "if the churches unite" or "if the theologians concur." If that were the case we would have to wait forever. God has declared that at a certain point, without our deserving it, meriting it or meeting prior conditions, He will intervene on behalf of His people by pouring out His Spirit upon all flesh. I believe we are living in precisely those days.

This final outpouring of the Holy Spirit is to lead right into the return of the Lord Jesus Christ, and it will be a universal outpouring. There was a great and wonderful move of the Holy Spirit in the early Church, but it did not reach all flesh. We have seen God do many wonderful works, but I believe they are nothing more than a drop in the bucket in comparison with what God will do in fulfillment of what He has here declared.

Four Stages

God's divine intervention at the close of this age is further spoken of in the book of Acts. Peter, preaching to the crowds after the healing of a lame man, declares:

> Repent therefore and be converted, that your sins may be blotted out, so that times of refreshing may come from the presence of the Lord, and that He may send Jesus Christ, who was preached to you before, whom heaven must receive until the times of restoration of all things, which God has spoken by the mouth of all His holy prophets since the world began.
>
> Acts 3:19–21

In his sermon, Peter gives a revelation of four stages that will bring the present age to its close:

First, God's people repent and turn back to Him.

Second, there are times of refreshing.

Third, there are times of restoration.

And, fourth, we have the return of Christ.

The first stage Peter describes is *repentance*. Before God can send a major visitation of divine grace, one step is always required—and that is the repentance of God's people. We see this principle in the slogan of Evan Roberts in the great revival that swept Wales and moved the world in 1904: "Bend the Church and bow the world." The problem is not bowing the world; it is bending the Church. If God can get His way with His people, He can get His way anywhere.

This principle of repentance is illustrated by the first coming of Jesus Christ. Jesus had a divinely appointed forerunner, John the Baptist, who prepared the way for His coming. The message of John the Baptist could be summed up in one word:

repent. Until the hearts of God's people had been prepared by this message, the Messiah could not be revealed. Judgment must begin at the house of God, and this is the message of the end times. If God's people will repent and turn back to Him, then will come the second stage: times of refreshing.

In the New King James Version the word *times* in the Scripture quoted above means a specific season like spring or fall. It is God's intent to give His people beautiful spiritual spring seasons of renewing and refreshing. We all enjoy the spring season when everything begins to turn green, the flowers return and life comes back to creation. These seasons of refreshing have visited the Church throughout its history, but they have been restricted to local areas and for limited periods of time.

In my understanding of God's end-time purposes, the outpouring to come will be the last and greatest outpouring of the Holy Spirit upon the Church of Jesus Christ. The purpose is to lead to the third stage: the times of restoration of all things. Here, the word *times* does not refer to a season but to a more extended or undefined period of time. Notice that Peter says "which God has spoken by the mouth of all His holy prophets since the world began." This period of restoration will be the climax of the age, which has been prophesied by every prophet God has ever placed in the world.

Restore, as I understand it, means "to put things back in their right place and their right condition." This is the message of the hour. God is putting His people back in their right place and in their right condition.

The restoration of the Church is going to bring us to the final stage, the ultimate climax of the age—with God sending Jesus Christ, whom heaven must receive and, by implication, retain, until this period of restoration of all things.

These four stages are God's program for closing this age. We will not focus on each stage in detail because it is outside the scope of this study. We will, however, consider the third stage, the times of restoration, at some depth. Why? Because that restoration relates directly to the Church and her victory over Satan's kingdom in the final conflict.

10

Restoration of the Church

In God's plan of restoration, what lies ahead for the Church? To answer that question, our next few chapters will focus on four phases of preparation within the Church for what God actually wants it to do. Then we will consider the three final objectives for the Church to achieve before this age closes.

The four preparatory stages God has planned for the Church do not need to take place in any particular order and may occur somewhat simultaneously.

First, God's people regroup around the Holy Spirit's up-lifted standard of Jesus Christ.

Second, God's people are delivered from demonic influence.

Third, God's people are re-equipped with the supernatural power of the Spirit.

And, fourth, God's people are regathered and joined together in a unified body.

The Uplifted Standard

To introduce the first phase of God's preparation of the Church, we look at Isaiah 59:19, which is a wonderful promise of God's grace for His people: "When the enemy comes in like a flood, the Spirit of the LORD will lift up a standard against him."

Just at the time God's people need Him most, when the enemy is pressing hardest and gaining ground in every area, God says that "the Spirit of the Lord will lift up a standard" against the enemy. If we look at the situation in much of the world, any reasonable Christian would have to acknowledge that since the end of World War II, the enemy has come in like a flood in most nations. This incursion has taken place in every major area of national life: the church, the seminaries, the educational systems, in political life, in moral and ethical standards, and in the economic systems. In so many areas of our world civilization, it is no exaggeration to say that the enemy, Satan, and all his works of darkness have come in like a flood.

My purpose in making this point is not to emphasize what the devil is doing. If, however, we acknowledge that the enemy has come in like a flood, then on the positive side we recognize that this is the moment for divine intervention. The Spirit of the Lord is now lifting up the standard.

In this present season, there is a sovereign, divine intervention by the Holy Spirit in the Church of Jesus Christ around the world. This passage from Isaiah 59:19, therefore, is one of the key verses of Scripture for us to consider in these days.

Jesus, the Standard

The Holy Spirit has only one standard to lift up. It is not a doctrine, a denomination, an institution or a special movement. It is a Person: the Lord Jesus Christ. Jesus said:

"When He, the Spirit of truth, has come, He will guide you into all truth; for He will not speak on His own authority, but whatever He hears He will speak; and He will tell you things to come. He will glorify Me, for He will take of what is Mine and declare it to you."

John 16:13–14

The supreme purpose of the Holy Spirit is to interpret and reveal all aspects of Jesus Christ in such a way as to glorify and magnify Him. The only person whom the Holy Spirit will ever exalt or uplift is the Son of God. One simple statement that typifies this standard is Hebrews 13:8: "Jesus Christ is the same yesterday, today, and forever."

I believe this principle is precisely what the Holy Spirit is saying to the Church: *Jesus Christ has not changed*. Nothing has been diminished from His glory, His faithfulness or His power. He is still the Savior from sin, the healer of the body, the baptizer in the Holy Spirit and the deliverer from demonic power. Jesus is still the head over all things to the Church. Nothing has changed in His position as the ultimate standard. Thankfully, the Holy Spirit is enabling us to see and acknowledge Him afresh.

Raising the Standard

Standards have been an important part of military units extending from the time of ancient armies all the way into our present day. During World War II, I was associated for two years with a group of British soldiers in the North African desert who were known as the Desert Rats. They became quite famous and even had a television program produced about them. Their standard was a little animal called a jerboa—a desert rat—which each soldier wore in a patch of white on his left sleeve. This symbol meant a great deal to those men, and it became a distinguished and honorable standard in those circles.

In ancient armies, the standard-bearer was a key person. Every group of soldiers was trained to identify, acknowledge and respect its own particular standard, which may have been an eagle, a leopard or a banner of some sort. If at any time that group of soldiers was being overrun by the enemy or was in danger of defeat, its commander would order the standard-bearer to an elevated piece of ground that could be seen from all directions. There he would lift up the standard, and all the soldiers, as they were trained, would regroup around it. This is exactly what is happening in the Church in our present day.

Isaiah 10 describes the total defeat of an invading Assyrian army, which came against Judah and Jerusalem. Their defeat by the supernatural intervention of God was summed up in Isaiah 10:18: "And they shall be as when a standard-bearer fainteth" (KJV). When the standard-bearer faints there is nothing for the soldiers to rally around. Without the standard, discouragement and defeat are almost inevitable.

I thank the Lord that the standard-bearer of God's people is the Holy Spirit, and with Him there is no fainting or weakness. He does not sleep or become lax in His duty. In our day the great Commander-in-Chief is telling the standard-bearer to lift up the standard. Again, this standard is not a particular teaching, movement or person. It is the Lord Jesus Christ.

Loyal to Jesus

There is a great rearrangement taking place among the people of God. Some people are more loyal to a movement, a leader or a doctrinal position than to the cause of Christ. The only believers who are going to gather around the signal of the Holy Spirit, therefore, are those whose primary loyalty is to the Lord Jesus Christ. The Holy Spirit is lifting up the standard, Jesus. God's defeated, discouraged and scattered people are receiving fresh hope as they rally around a restored vision of His glory.

In reality, God has no other rallying point for His people. A prophecy about the Messiah coming from the tribe of Judah says: "The scepter shall not depart from Judah, nor a lawgiver from between his feet, until Shiloh comes; and to Him shall be the obedience of the people" (Genesis 49:10).

Most Bible commentators agree that *Shiloh* is a name of the Messiah. In Hebrew the name means "the one to whom it belongs." There is only one focal point for the gathering of God's people, and that is the Lord Jesus Christ, the Messiah. He is Shiloh, the one to whom we belong. He is the standard—the foundation and the head of the Church.

11

Delivered from Demons

In our previous chapter, we explored the first of four preparatory stages God has planned for the Church in these times: God's people regrouping around the Lord Jesus Christ, the standard lifted up by the Holy Spirit.

In this chapter, we will examine the second phase of the preparation of the Church. This stage, as I understand it, involves Christians being delivered from an invading army of "insects" or evil spirits that have destroyed the inheritance of God's people through the centuries.

I believe this invasion is pictured prophetically by the prophet Joel. Two trees symbolize two peoples to whom God is committed by a covenant that He will not break. I believe the fig tree talked about in the book of Joel symbolizes Israel and the vine symbolizes the Church.

Total Desolation

With this symbolism in mind, let's look at the first chapter of Joel. It gives us a picture of total desolation inflicted by an invading army of insects: "What the chewing locust left, the swarming locust has eaten; what the swarming locust left, the crawling locust has eaten; and what the crawling locust left, the consuming locust has eaten" (Joel 1:4).

The result of the invasion by these insects is summed up in Joel 1:12: "The vine has dried up, and the fig tree has withered; . . . joy has withered away from the sons of men." God is moving today to meet this need within the Church. The Lord is delivering His people from the demonic spirits that have eaten away at the very root of their joy, peace and liberty.

How do demons gnaw away at the joy of God's people? They bring fear and frustration, defeat and poverty, sickness and infirmity, despair and suicide, resentment and hatred. How has this happened? It takes place when God's people become followers of external religious customs that are devoid of internal reality. Doctrines can be strong in theory—but not in experience. Sometimes the people singing hymns about joy and peace look so worried and miserable that one might wonder how they could even get those words out of their mouths. In reality, the more you have in doctrine, the greater your frustration can be if you do not have it in experience.

Parts of the Church are experiencing this kind of desolation. Fortunately, beside a picture of desolation, Joel also gives us a wonderful promise of God's restoration: "So I will restore to you the years that the swarming locust has eaten, the crawling locust, the consuming locust, and the chewing locust, My great army which I sent among you" (Joel 2:25).

God has allowed this invading army of demons because the Church began to look to standards other than the Lord Jesus. The great promise of restoration continues with the outpouring of the Holy Spirit: "And it shall come to pass afterward that I will pour out My Spirit on all flesh" (Joel 2:28).

The Promise of Deliverance

The results of this outpouring are summed up in Joel 2:32: "It shall come to pass that whoever calls on the name of the Lord shall be saved [delivered, KJV]." The outpoured Spirit makes it possible for believers to receive deliverance from the invading army.

There is a beautiful, succinct summary of the order of this deliverance in the book of Obadiah. *Zion* is one of Scripture's names for God's people, both natural and spiritual as Israel and the Church: "But on Mount Zion there shall be deliverance, and there shall be holiness; the house of Jacob shall possess their possessions" (Obadiah 1:17).

Obadiah presents an order of restoration that we cannot reverse. Before God's people can appropriate their possessions and regain their inheritance, there must be deliverance. First, we must get the "insects" out. Second, there must be holiness. God is a holy God; the Bible is His holy Word; the Spirit of God is a *holy* Spirit. And, therefore, God's people are called to live holy lives. There is no inheritance in Christ for the unholy.

Jesus told the apostle Paul, "That they may receive . . . an inheritance among those who are sanctified [made holy] by faith in Me" (Acts 26:18). God is a holy God and He has not varied His requirements for holiness from age to age or from generation to generation. Everything in Scripture tells us that to approach God we must learn the lessons of holiness. The order is first holiness, then the possession of our inheritance.

The third aspect of this promise is: "The house of Jacob shall possess their possessions." It is one thing to *have* possessions; it is another thing to *possess* them. Consider this in light of the nation of Israel. According to Scripture they have owned their land in God's sight for the last two thousand years. For most of that time, however, they have not been near it. They have *had* their possession, but they did not *possess* it.

The same is true of much of the Christian Church today. Legally, in Christ, we have owned our inheritance all along, but we have not possessed it.

Some people say, "I got it all when I was born again."

My answer is, "If you got it all, let's see it all!"

Step by Step

It is absolutely true that we did inherit everything in Christ the moment we were born again. Most people, however, do not possess it experientially except the hard way—step by step and battle by battle. God commanded Joshua, "Now therefore, arise, go over this Jordan, you and all this people, to the land which I am giving to them—the children of Israel. Every place that the sole of your foot will tread upon I have given you" (Joshua 1:2–3).

When God spoke this command to Joshua, the Israelites had not put one foot on the ground in the land of promise. Yes, that land was theirs legally because God said, "I am giving the land to them." To possess it, however, they had to take it experientially by warfare. They had the legal claim, but they had to assert that claim in the face of every opposition.

It is a good thing Joshua and the children of Israel were not like many modern Christians. When God said, "I've given it to you," the children of Israel, like some believers today, could have folded their arms, stood on the east bank of the Jordan River and said, "Praise the Lord, it's all ours. We got it all!" Had they done that, the Canaanites would have laughed in their faces.

Here is the reality: You do not have more than you have possessed. You and I can, however, possess our inheritance if we go about it God's way: deliverance, holiness and then possessing our possessions. Deliverance of God's people from the invading army of demonic spirits is the necessary prelude to the rest of that process.

12

Re-Equipping

We have covered the first two preparatory stages for the Church in our day—the promise of the Holy Spirit lifting up Jesus as the standard, and the necessity of deliverance of God's people from invading demonic entities. Now we turn to the third phase of preparation: God's people being *re-equipped*.

Let's begin with the wonderful promises cited in Acts 2:17–18:

> "And it shall come to pass in the last days, says God, that I will pour out of My Spirit on all flesh; your sons and your daughters shall prophesy, your young men shall see visions, your old men shall dream dreams. And on My menservants and on My maidservants I will pour out My Spirit in those days; and they shall prophesy."

When the Holy Spirit is poured out, the gifts of the Spirit are restored. The Holy Spirit generously provides what the

Church needs—gifts of visions and revelation, the gifts of power and the ministry of prophecy. When this happens, God's people begin to have something substantive to exercise. They have something tangible to demonstrate the power of God to the world.

Supernatural Tools

God's people are beginning to receive again the tools that are needed to reap the harvest and defeat the kingdom of darkness. It would be ridiculous to send forth reapers into the harvest field without a sickle, or to send soldiers into battle without a weapon. In recognition of this need, God's intention is to restore to His people the gifts of the Holy Spirit. They are the tools and weapons that are needed for doing the work. Paul made this comment about his ministry in Romans 15:18–19:

> For I will not dare to speak of any of those things which Christ has not accomplished through me, in word and deed, to make the Gentiles obedient—in mighty signs and wonders, by the power of the Spirit of God, so that from Jerusalem and round about to Illyricum I have fully preached the gospel of Christ.

It is my firm conviction that the stubborn, rebellious, unbelieving heart of man will never be brought into full subjection to the Gospel of Jesus Christ without the demonstration of supernatural power. I have seen this connection confirmed numerous times. Most of the time, you can get a degree of conformity, acceptance of doctrine and church membership without really changing attitudes or hearts. It often takes the demonstrated supernatural power of God to make men and women really obedient. One miracle has the power to make even the most obstinate person tremble.

The Power of God

The miraculous is necessary; it is not optional. Paul could not have said, "I fully preach the Gospel," if he had not demonstrated the power of God. Paul writes:

> And I, brethren, when I came to you, did not come with excellence of speech or of wisdom declaring to you the testimony of God. For I determined not to know anything among you except Jesus Christ and Him crucified. I was with you in weakness, in fear, and in much trembling. And my speech and my preaching were not with persuasive words of human wisdom, but in demonstration of the Spirit and of power, that your faith should not be in the wisdom of men but in the power of God.
>
> 1 Corinthians 2:1–5

We have a choice: Are we going to put our faith in the wisdom of human beings or in the supernatural power of God? Those who put their faith in education and learning never have a solid foundation for their faith. Those who have tasted the power of God by personal experience, however, have seen the verification of His Word. They know personally the One in whom they have believed. I have seen this demonstrated again and again. Real faith must be based on the supernatural power of God.

In the last resort, the intellectual approach will always undermine the faith of God's people. This is precisely what has happened in the Church for many decades. Many intellectually trained professors and seminarians are perfectly sincere, but, as Billy Graham said, it is possible to be sincere and be sincerely wrong.

God has not asked the ministers of the Church of Jesus Christ to sit in judgment of the Word of God; we are to demonstrate it. The Gospel is not a set of theories; it is the remedy for human need. When humanity sees their need met through the Gospel, then they will obey it.

13

Regathering

Up to this point we have discussed the first three preparatory phases for the end-times Church: the activity of the Holy Spirit to lift up Jesus as the standard, deliverance from demonic armies, and re-equipping through the gifts of the Spirit. Now we come to the fourth preparatory phase: God's people being regathered and joined together in a unified body.

A vivid Old Testament picture for this phase is found in Ezekiel's vision in the valley of dry bones. It is a prophecy of the restoration and regathering of God's people, which applies to the nation of Israel. I believe, however, that it is also a picture of the regathering of the scattered members of Christ's Body, the Church. Personally, my belief is that in the sight of God, the Church has been like Israel: dry bones scattered around, unconnected, unattached, without knowing their places, and without knowing their functions in the body.

Getting Involved

The process of regathering began when the Lord engaged Ezekiel, asking him a penetrating question.

God said to Ezekiel, "Can these bones live?"

Ezekiel replied, "O Lord God, You know."

I marvel at the grace of God because He could have accomplished His plan without Ezekiel. Instead, He said, "Ezekiel, I want you to prophesy, and when you prophesy things will start to happen." Amazingly, the Lord invites us to share in His plan and purposes.

> So I [Ezekiel] prophesied as I was commanded; and as I prophesied, there was a noise, and suddenly a rattling; and the bones came together, bone to bone. Indeed, as I looked, the sinews and the flesh came upon them, and the skin covered them over; but there was no breath in them. Also He said to me, "Prophesy to the breath, prophesy, son of man, and say to the breath, 'Thus says the Lord GOD: "Come from the four winds, O breath, and breathe on these slain, that they may live."'" So I prophesied as He commanded me, and breath [Hebrew, spirit] came into them, and they lived, and stood upon their feet, an exceedingly great army.
>
> Ezekiel 37:7–10

By the time God had finished His work, the scattered bones had become a great army. Today God is again bringing forth an army out of the scattered bones. In the process there is a lot of noise, shaking and disturbance. Some people are saying, "Don't rock the boat." God, however, has created the noise and rattling to shake His people out of their complacency.

Coming Together

People who are being touched by God's Spirit are beginning to move. Bones are coming to bones and people are committing themselves to their places in the Body of Christ.

In his first letter to the Corinthians, Paul gives this instruction to the Church:

> For as the body is one and has many members, but all the members of that one body, being many, are one body, so also is Christ. . . . For in fact the body is not one member but many. If the foot should say, "Because I am not a hand, I am not of the body," is it therefore not of the body? . . . And the eye cannot say to the hand, "I have no need of you"; nor again the head to the feet, "I have no need of you."
>
> 1 Corinthians 12:12, 14–15, 21

Paul is telling us we need one another. Since that is true, we must be rightly related to one another and be properly fitted together. This is the final phase that prepares the Church to confront the powers of darkness. Paul pictures this in Ephesians 4:16. Speaking about Christ as the head of the Church, he writes: "From whom the whole body, joined and knit together by what every joint supplies, according to the effective working by which every part does its share, causes growth of the body for the edifying of itself in love."

Please notice in this passage that the body edifies the body. This can only happen when every part is in the right place, properly fitted together with the other parts, and properly fulfilling its function.

Shining Forth

Now let's look at a glorious picture of God's people after restoration.

> Arise, shine; for your light has come! And the glory of the LORD is risen upon you. For behold, the darkness shall cover the earth, and deep darkness the people; but the LORD will

arise over you, and His glory will be seen upon you. The Gentiles [the nations] shall come to your light, and kings to the brightness of your rising. "Lift up your eyes all around, and see: They all gather together, they come to you; your sons shall come from afar, and your daughters shall be nursed at your side. Then you shall see and become radiant, and your heart shall swell with joy; because the abundance of the sea shall be turned to you, the wealth of the Gentiles shall come to you."

Isaiah 60:1–5

This gives us an idea of what God is intending to do in these last days—and we have a part in it. First of all, we have a choice in our outlook. We can look at the negative or we can look at the positive. The negative is "darkness shall cover the earth, and deep darkness the people." That is manifestly true, and it is going to become even more true the nearer we come to the close of this age. For negative-minded persons, all they will be able to speak about is what the devil is doing, and how the world is getting worse and worse.

That is all true, but it is not the whole truth. The other part of the truth is: "Arise, shine; for your light has come!" At the moment when darkness covers the earth and deep darkness covers the people, the true people of God are going to shine forth. We will move forward with a light and a glory that the world has never before seen upon us.

"Then nations are going to come to your light, and kings to the brightness of your rising." One day we may see whole nations—along with their leaders—turn to the Lord Jesus Christ by the supernatural moving of the Spirit of God. I believe Scripture declares it will happen. "Nations will come to your light and kings to the brightness of your rising." It is becoming increasingly obvious that political leaders today have very few answers to the political, environmental and economic problems the world is facing. If a group would come forth and be able to demonstrate workable answers to the world's problems, they would have presidents and prime ministers waiting at their doors.

In the 1930s William Branham was just a simple preacher from a small town in Kentucky. But in 1950 King George VI, ruler of the great British Empire, sent for Branham because he had heard that Branham had something the doctors did not have: a powerful ministry of healing that became known worldwide. When people see that God heals cancer and blind eyes, the wealthiest and the most famous in the land will be the ones waiting in line. When the light shines, the world will come.

The prophet Isaiah further declares: "The abundance of the sea shall be turned to you, the wealth of the Gentiles shall come to you." I have been praying for the wealth of the United States to be converted to the purposes of God in this generation. I believe God gave me that prayer, and I have prayed it in the name of Jesus. The Bible says if I ask anything in His name, He will do it. This nation has a destiny with unique privileges, potentialities and opportunities. Why leave all those resources in the hand of the devil? God says, "The silver is mine, and the gold is mine, saith the Lord of hosts. The glory of this latter house shall be greater than of the former'" (Haggai 2:8–9 KJV).

When you ask the Lord for silver and gold, you are not stealing. Actually, the devil is the one who stole it. It does not belong to him; it belongs to God. That wealth should be used for glorifying the house of God, which is the true Church of Jesus Christ.

The Sun of Righteousness

Another Scripture, Song of Solomon 6:10, gives us one more glimpse of the true Church emerging from the darkness of night: "Who is she who looks forth as the morning, fair as the moon, clear as the sun, awesome as an army with banners?"

This describes how the Church is going to appear at the close of this age. She will have the beauty of the moon reflecting the sun, which is Jesus. She will be as terrible to all the forces of darkness as an army with banners. God is bringing us together as His Body so that we may be an exceedingly great army, equipped for war and for the fulfillment of God's purposes.

The last chapter of the Old Testament, Malachi 4, relates to the close of the age. The first verse speaks about the day of God's judgment and is followed in verse 2 with a promise for God's people: "For behold, the day is coming, burning like an oven, and all the proud, yes, all who do wickedly will be stubble. . . . But to you who fear My name the Sun of Righteousness shall arise with healing in His wings."

I believe this is a promise for our generation. The Church is at the end of the long night of apostasy and unbelief. At this strategic moment, the Sun of Righteousness, Jesus Christ, is going to rise with healing in His wings. I believe we will see tremendous revivals of healing within the Body of Christ in the days ahead. The two great products of the Gospel are righteousness and healing. The Gospel brings deliverance from sin and deliverance from sickness. God's people are going to go forth and trample underfoot the forces of the enemy.

We see a similar thought in Romans 16:20. It contains this beautiful promise for us: "And the God of peace will crush Satan under your feet shortly." This promise has yet to be fulfilled. It was written to believers in Jesus Christ.

The healing that comes is not going to be just the healing of individual physical bodies. It is going to be the healing of the collective Body of Jesus Christ as well.

As I close this chapter, I want to share one final, beautiful promise.

> Moreover the light of the moon will be as the light of the sun, and the light of the sun will be sevenfold, as the light of seven days, in the day that the LORD binds up the bruise of His people and heals the stroke of their wound.
>
> Isaiah 30:26

A day is approaching when God will heal the bruises of His people and the stroke of their wounds. It is going to be a day of extreme brightness and glory. It will be the time when the Sun of Righteousness arises with healing in His wings.

14

The Church's Final Purpose

In our previous chapters, we have explored the four preparatory stages for the Church in our day: regrouping around the Holy Spirit's uplifted standard of Jesus Christ, deliverance from demonic enemy invaders, re-equipping for greater effectiveness, and regathering in unity. The result is a stronger, more glorious Church.

As God restores the Church to the glory for which she was created, He has three main objectives for her to accomplish at the close of the age.

First is the ingathering of the last great harvest.

Second is the preparation of the Church as Bride for the Bridegroom, Jesus Christ.

Third is the restraining and final casting down of Satan's kingdom.

The Latter Rain

First, the Church is to be the instrument of the ingathering of the final great harvest at the consummation of the age. In Deuteronomy we read a principle of God's provision that is consistent throughout the Word. Here is the principle: Rain is always given for the sake of the harvest. God gave His people this assurance before He brought them into the Promised Land. He told them that if they were obedient, the rain and the harvest would never fail (see Leviticus 26:3–4). God promised specifically: "Then I will give you the rain for your land in its season, the early rain and the latter rain, that you may gather in your grain, your new wine, and your oil" (Deuteronomy 11:14).

The theme of the early and latter rains follows throughout Scripture. The first (or early) rain at the beginning of the winter initiates the growing season in Israel. The latter rain at the end of the winter brings the crops to maturity and immediately precedes the final processes of harvest. Three aspects of restoration within God's people are represented in this process: the grain of the Word, the wine of joy and the oil of the Holy Spirit.

I believe the outpouring of the Holy Spirit throughout the history of the Church corresponds to the way God ordained for the rains to come in the land of Israel. First, the early rain began the winter growing season. The early rain of the Holy Spirit fell on the Church beginning on the day of Pentecost and continued to be poured out for a century or more.

Most church historians agree that after the close of the first century, the Holy Spirit did not move in such a universal way for many centuries. During those centuries there were moves of the Holy Spirit that brought new life to the specific churches or areas. But, like the winter rains in Israel, these moves were sporadic and unpredictable.

Following this season, the latter rain is to be the last great, all-inclusive outpouring of the Holy Spirit. This latter rain is designed by God to bring the harvest at the close of the age to maturity.

It is my personal conviction that the latter rain began to fall again upon the Church at the beginning of the twentieth century. Like the latter rain in Israel, this outpouring of the Holy Spirit has been universal, touching practically every nation on earth either directly or indirectly. It has embraced all sections of the Church—affecting every denomination in one way or another. In my understanding of God's end-time purposes, this latter rain will be the last and greatest outpouring of the Holy Spirit upon the Church of Jesus Christ.

This outpouring is given so that the harvest may be gathered in. Some, however, resist this outpouring. As we see from the verse below, it is the mark of a defiant and rebellious heart that fails to see that God is giving rain. Tragically, this is the case in many sections of the Church today.

> But this people has a defiant and rebellious heart; they have revolted and departed. They do not say in their heart, "Let us now fear the LORD our God, who gives rain, both the former and the latter, in its season. He reserves for us the appointed weeks of the harvest."
>
> Jeremiah 5:23–24

Harvest Time

Scripture says, however, that in spite of the hardness of many hearts, God in His faithfulness will give the rain in His season. He will pour out the former and the latter rain, because He has reserved the appointed weeks of the harvest. God has kept His hand over that period of time at the close of the age when the earth's harvest must be reaped. It cannot be brought in, however, until both the former and the latter rain have been poured out.

> Therefore be patient, brethren, until the coming of the Lord. See how the farmer waits for the precious fruit of the earth, waiting patiently for it until it receives the early and latter rain. You also be patient. Establish your hearts, for the coming of the Lord is at hand.
>
> James 5:7–8

The farmer cannot gather in the harvest until he has received both the early and the latter rain. Even so, immediately after that latter rain falls, the next item on the agenda is the gathering of the harvest. Just as there were "appointed weeks of the harvest" in Israel, I believe the harvest is a specific period in God's dispensational dealings with His Church.

In the Old Testament, the Passover feast is a "type" of Calvary—carrying specific symbolism about what Jesus accomplished there. Commonly, such a "type" is a picture using a person, event or specific item to present some particular aspect of Old Testament truth that is revealed fully in the New Testament. Just as the Feast of Pentecost under the Old Covenant was fulfilled on the Day of Pentecost in the New, there is a third great feast that has yet to be fulfilled. Under the Old Covenant, every Jewish male had to go up to Jerusalem every year for the Feast of Harvest. This feast has a counterpart in the Church age just as the other two great feasts had. This feast will be fulfilled at the close of this age when the last great harvest of souls is gathered in all around the earth.

This harvest is what God is working toward in the pouring out of the rain of the Holy Spirit. His purpose in giving His Spirit is not for spiritual self-indulgence—to create little "bless me clubs." It is given to equip and send forth workers into the fields to reap the last harvest of the earth.

In Jesus' great prophetic discourse unfolding the course of events for the close of the age, He provided the sign of His coming: "And this gospel of the kingdom will be preached in all the world as a witness to all the nations, and then the end will come" (Matthew 24:14).

The disciples had asked, "What will be the sign of your coming and the end of the age?" They had asked a specific question to which He had given a specific answer: "this gospel of the kingdom." It was not to be a watered-down gospel, but the total Gospel of the Kingdom of God preached in all the world for a witness to all nations. This is the reaping of the last great harvest for which God is preparing His Church.

Preparing the Bride

God's second great objective for the Church at the close of the age is the preparation of the Church as a Bride to meet her Bridegroom. Ephesians 5:25–27 is a description of the marriage relationship between husband and wife. But it applies also to the Church.

> Husbands, love your wives, just as Christ also loved the church and gave Himself for her, that He might sanctify and cleanse her with the washing of water by the word, that He might present her to Himself a glorious church, not having spot or wrinkle or any such thing, but that she should be holy and without blemish.

The Lord is not coming for a withered, wrinkled old hag who is hobbling around with a cane. He is coming for a holy, beautiful and active bride. He will not present Himself with anything less than the best. In that regard, one of the great functions of the Holy Spirit in the Church is to make the Church ready.

The process is to take place through the sanctifying and cleansing with the washing of water by the Word. Christians who do not submit to the disciplines of the Word cannot expect to be included in this company. Revelation 19:7 brings out the same truth as well: "Let us be glad and rejoice and give Him glory, for the marriage of the Lamb has come, and His wife has made herself ready."

At His coming, the Church will not *be making* herself ready. She *has made* herself ready. The true Church is getting ready, with all the expectations of a bride looking for the coming of her bridegroom. If you think of the anticipation and excitement in the heart of a young lady as the day of the marriage approaches—and also the longing in the heart of the young man—you can better understand the relationship between the true Church and Jesus Christ at the close of this age. His desire is toward His Bride, and His Bride's desire is toward Him. Nothing will ever be more important to either of them than the other. This is the Church for which Jesus is coming.

First John 3:3 says, "Everyone who has this hope in Him purifies himself, just as He is pure." The real evidence of our hope for the coming of the Lord is that we have individually purified ourselves with the washing of the water by the Word. We are cleansed by hearing, receiving and obeying the Word of God—by seeking after and doing His commandments.

Jesus said, "He who has My commandments and keeps them, it is he who loves Me" (John 14:21). If you do not care to seek after the commandments of the Lord or you are not willing to obey them, you will not be part of this company.

Casting Down Satan

The third objective for the Church to accomplish at the end of the age is restraining and casting down Satan's kingdom. The apostle Paul writes, "The weapons of our warfare are not carnal but mighty in God for pulling down strongholds, casting down arguments and every high thing that exalts itself against the knowledge of God" (2 Corinthians 10:4–5).

This describes the entire kingdom of Satan, which is to be cast down by the spiritual weapons committed to the people of God. The spiritual weapons to dethrone Satan are in the hands of God's people. We must now have the diligence and courage to use them.

In a later chapter, I am going to deal with the specific topic of our authority as the Church to restrain and cast down Satan. Then, in the final chapters, we will study the spiritual weapons committed to us and how they are to be exercised.

First, however, it is helpful if we understand the structure of the kingdom of darkness that we will be opposing. Also, it will help us to understand that Satan has a plan for the close of the age just as God does. As in earthly warfare, a general engaging in battle has an advantage if he knows the plans of his enemy. In the same way, as we understand Satan's plan for the close of the age, we are better prepared to overthrow it and cast it down.

15

The Opposing Kingdom

As God prepares the Body of Christ for the end times, He is doing a work of restoration among His people and in His Church. The result will be a Church that is renewed, united, equipped and empowered to go forth and fulfill the task God has committed to His people.

In opposition to God's work of restoration, Satan also has a kingdom and a plan for the close of this age, just as God does. Everything God does Satan tries to counterfeit, because he does not have the power to create anything on his own. Only God can create.

One of God's final objectives for the restored Church is the restraining and casting down of Satan's kingdom. We need, therefore, to consider what the Bible has to say about the structure of Satan's kingdom as well as his strategy for trying to control the entire world in the end times. In this chapter we will look at the structure of his kingdom.

Two Kingdoms at War

References to two opposing kingdoms are placed side by side in Colossians 1:12–14:

> Giving thanks to the Father who has qualified us to be partakers of the inheritance of the saints in the light. He has delivered us from the power of darkness and conveyed us into the kingdom of the Son of His love, in whom we have redemption through His blood, the forgiveness of sins.

In this passage we see the two kingdoms: one, the domain of darkness; the other, the Kingdom of the Son of God's love. We are either in one kingdom or in the other. There is no middle ground and no neutrality. Redemption through the blood of Jesus is the basis of our deliverance from the kingdom of Satan into the Kingdom of God.

The Present World Order

Scripture tells us who belongs in Satan's kingdom. Very simply, Satan's kingdom contains all who are disobedient to God. All who are in rebellion against God are automatically in Satan's kingdom. They do not make a decision or have a vote.

> And you He [God] made alive, who were dead [spiritually] in trespasses and sins, in which you once walked according to the course of this world, according to the prince of the power of the air, the spirit who now works in the sons of disobedience, among whom also we all once conducted ourselves in the lusts of our flesh, fulfilling the desires of the flesh and of the mind, and were by nature children of wrath, just as the others.
>
> Ephesians 2:1–3

The *world* in this passage is this present age—not the world as the created earth, but the world as the present world order. Second Peter 3:6, for instance, says that in Noah's flood, the world that existed at that time perished. It is clear that the earth itself did not perish. Rather, the whole human order of that day perished. The *world* is this present world order involving all humanity and all nations. Each of us was once very much a part of that world order—every one of us.

Paul writes that those who are part of this world order walk "according to the prince of the power of the air." The Greek word for *prince* is *arche*, which means "a ruler." This occurs in English words such as *archangel* or *archbishop*—an archangel being a ruling angel and an archbishop a ruling bishop. The ruler of the power (Greek, authority) of the air is Satan. He is the ruler of the realm of authority defined by the "air."

There are two Greek words for air. One is *aither*, which gives us the English word *ether*. The other is *aer*, which gives us the English word *air*. There is a difference. *Aither* is the upper atmosphere, while *aer*, or air, is the lower, denser atmosphere contiguous with the earth's surface.

Aer is the word that is used in this verse, meaning that Satan is the ruler of the realm of authority that takes in the whole surface of the earth. How did he become ruler? It happened because God's appointed ruler, Adam, betrayed this realm of authority to him. Satan tricked his way into this position, usurping it from Adam. But the authority is ultimately from God.

Notice that Satan is depicted in this verse as a spirit. He is not a fleshly being, but a spiritual being who is now at work in the "sons of disobedience." The key word here is *disobedience*. Everybody who is disobedient to God is under the influence of Satan. Paul goes on to say, "Among whom also we all had once conducted ourselves [all of us; there are no exceptions] in the lusts of our flesh, fulfilling the desires of the flesh and of the mind."

Mind Your Mind

Before we came to Christ, we were motivated by our fleshly nature and by our minds. Be aware that the mind is just as much at enmity against God as the carnal nature. Paul says in Romans 8:7 that the carnal, unredeemed, unregenerate mind "is enmity against God." Most people can see that the obvious fleshly sins are at enmity with God. But actually, the mind in many ways is more at enmity with God than the carnal nature.

While ministering in Stockholm, Sweden, many years ago, I was asked to conduct a deliverance service. Actually the service ended up being somewhat comical. I was allowed to teach in the church, where the general meetings were held, but they felt it was not appropriate for me to minister deliverance there. That part of the service would be conducted in a small room a short distance away from the actual church building.

After I finished teaching, I asked for all those who felt they needed deliverance to move to the next room. Practically the whole congregation moved. In this packed setting, I instructed the people how to pray. Then I began to command the evil spirits to come out, and things got rather exciting. I remember a Swedish Pentecostal pastor squeezing his way around the room, looking at members of his congregation who were being delivered from evil spirits. He kept remarking, "I don't believe what I'm seeing."

Afterward some of the Christians in Sweden who heard what had happened in that meeting sent a message to me saying how stupid it was to imagine that Swedes could need deliverance from evil spirits. Their rationale? Swedes are much too intellectual to need deliverance!

Here is the truth of the matter: The intellect is more at enmity with God than the fleshly old nature that gets drunk or commits immorality. The mind is really the ultimate portrait of rebellion against God. One of the results is that educating the carnal mind can often amount to educating an enemy of God. It is no accident that the main opposition to the Gospel is found in academic circles. Ironically, much of the strongest opposition can be found in some seminaries. Educating unregenerate minds is simply making them more antichrist in disposition than they were before.

Rebellious and Proud

This, then, is the nature of the world. It is the disobedient against God—those who are at enmity with God in their fleshly nature and in their minds. This overall antipathy is summed up in Ephesians 2:3 with the phrase *children of wrath*. The world system as it is described here is Satan's kingdom. He is a spiritual ruler who by spiritual power dominates the surface of the earth and those who are in rebellion against God. It is the rebellion of mankind that automatically causes people to be Satan's subjects.

Clearly, Satan is the arch rebel. As such, we see a vivid picture of him in Job 41. This amazing chapter is devoted to the description of a sea monster named Leviathan. I believe that Leviathan, like the serpent in the Garden, is not just a creature. It is also an embodiment of Satan. In fact, I do not think one can understand this chapter in any other way. In that respect, what is said in the last verse is extremely significant: "He [Leviathan] beholds every high thing; he is king over all the children of pride" (verse 34).

Satan is king over all the children of pride. It does not matter whether they are Baptists, charismatics, Catholics, Buddhists, Hindus or Communists. If there is pride, Satan is their king. Consider this question: Which came first, pride or rebellion? The answer is pride. Pride led to rebellion. The root of all problems in our nature is pride; consequently, we see that when God gets down to the root of pride, changes begin to happen.

Satan is the ruler over all the proud and rebellious. He is an invisible ruler who dominates, controls and manipulates them by his spiritual power.

Our Wrestling Match

Let's look again at the picture of Satan's kingdom given in Ephesians 6:12. We will cite the New King James Version and then I will give you my own personal version—the "Prince Version." Here is the NKJV: "For we do not wrestle against flesh and blood, but against principalities, against powers, against the rulers of the darkness of this age, against spiritual hosts of wickedness in the heavenly places."

I have sometimes commented that most Christians punctuate that verse incorrectly. They read it as: "For we do not wrestle"—period. The truth is, whether we want to wrestle or not, we must. Paul says we are in a wrestling match that is not against flesh and blood. It is very significant that Paul chose the metaphor of wrestling. Personally, I do not think it is a metaphor; I believe it is an actual fact. Wrestling is the most intense form of person-to-person contact.

Let me now give you "the Prince translation," which I have based on the Greek text. We begin with the first phrase: "For our wrestling match is not against persons with bodies." This wording also appears in *The Living Bible*, and I think it is excellent. Why? Because it brings out the fact that we are dealing with spiritual entities—persons who do not have bodies.

Once you have that truth clear in your understanding, you are way ahead in spiritual conflict. Many times when you encounter problems, if you believe you are just dealing with some psychological force inside yourself or some personal fixations, you have not come to grips with spiritual reality. You and I must realize we are dealing with unseen, wicked persons who do not have bodies and who hate us passionately.

As I mentioned earlier in this book, I wrestled for years with depression. It was only when I realized I was dealing with a person—an invisible, spiritual person—that I was finally and completely delivered. When I knew that I was dealing with a person, I was most of the way to victory.

That was in 1953. Ten years later, the Lord thrust me (against my own wishes, I might add) into the ministry of delivering others. I thought it was terrible for a minister to have to admit he was delivered from an evil spirit. In fact, the only person who ever knew about my experience was my first wife. The overall point is that we are dealing with persons without bodies. As soon as you realize that, you are in an altogether different position to handle it.

Almost all pagan religions know and recognize the reality of evil spirits. It is Christians who are, for the most part, ignorant. The sooner we recognize that our wrestling match is against rulerships (Greek, *arche*), powers and authorities, the better we will be able to deal with them.

A Malevolent Structure

Ephesians 6:12 also helps us realize that the evil we face has a structure and an order. The "Prince Version" of the latter portion of that verse is as follows: "rulerships with various areas and descending orders of authority." This means that there are rulers and sub-rulers. In the state of Hawaii, for example, on the largest island (which is also named Hawaii) there is without any question a satanic ruler over this island named Pele. You can ask the locals and discover that they have known this fact for centuries.

In this hierarchy of evil, under the various sub-rulers are lower sub-rulers who may be over major cities or even distinctive ethnic groups. The organization of Satan's kingdom is extremely effective because he got it from God. Remember, Lucifer was the arch ruler—the archangel—over one third of the angels. He turned those angels in rebellion against God, but he kept the structure of rulership. That is why his kingdom, with its various areas and descending orders of authority, is so efficient.

Here is the "Prince Version" of the next phrase: "the world dominators of this present darkness." Those words—*world* and *dominate*—are significant because they show Satan's aim to dominate the entire world. Because this is his purpose, everything Satan does is directed toward that end. As we will see in the next chapter, Satan's kingdom is a kingdom of darkness; consequently, those who are in it do not know where they are because they are in the dark.

The final phrase is: "spiritual [blank] of wickedness." Let me explain the "blank." The Greek language has a neuter gender that can be used in the plural without a noun. As a result, this can be translated "spirituals of wickedness." You cannot say that in English, so you have to add in some more specific words. The two words usually put in are *hosts* or *forces*. I prefer *hosts* because they are angels, as I understand it. That makes this phrase *spiritual hosts of wickedness*.

These forces are "the world dominators of this present darkness." The NKJV reads: "rulers of the darkness of this age." I prefer to use the word *dominate* because the Greek word *krato* is a powerful word. Actually, a form of this word is also used in the title of Jesus: *pantokrator*, which is translated "Almighty."

Paul uses another powerful word to describe the work of the hosts of darkness: *kosmokrator*. This word can be literally translated, "the dominators of the cosmos," referring to the cosmos as the present world order. There are two dirty words in the spiritual world. One is *dominate* and the other is *manipulate*. Wherever you encounter those terms, you have met Satan, for this is what our enemy loves to do. In stark contrast, God never dominates; He never manipulates.

The Heavenlies

Paul also tells us in Ephesians 6:12 that these spiritual hosts are "in the heavenly places." A literal translation would be "in the heavenlies." Remember that Satan's kingdom is made up of persons without bodies. I believe they are various angels structured in rulerships. There are various descending orders of authority, with each ruler being answerable to the ruler above him.

For some Christians, it may be problematic to think that Satan's headquarters can be in the heavenlies. Let me suggest here that from the first verse of the Bible, *heaven* is plural. In the beginning God created the "heavens" and the earth. Paul writes: "I know a man in Christ who fourteen years ago—whether in the body I do not know, or whether out of the body I do not know, God knows—such a one was caught up to the third heaven" (2 Corinthians 12:2). Logically, if there is a third heaven, there must be a first and a second.

Ephesians 4:10, speaking about the fact that Christ descended into Hades and then ascended into heaven, says: "He who descended is also the one who ascended far above all the heavens." When Paul says *all the heavens*, this phrase tells us the same thing as the conclusion drawn earlier. There must be more than one heaven. Some people talk about being in the "seventh heaven." Actually, I would recommend against Christians using this phrase, because it is taken from the Koran. If you are feeling really happy, my suggestion is to say you are on cloud nine!

The Bible leaves little doubt that Satan was cast out of the heaven of God's presence. Apparently, somewhere in between the heaven of God's presence and the earth, Satan set up a rival kingdom of rebellious angels. This is significant when we consider it in connection with our prayer life. Why? Because when we pray, we often must pierce through satanic opposition arranged against us. This is why we use the phrase *praying through*.

The presence of this satanic kingdom affects every Christian, because the moment you are born into the Kingdom of God, you are born into a Kingdom that is at war with Satan's kingdom. Whether we like it or not, we will experience that conflict. By way of illustration, I am a naturalized

American citizen. Suppose that when I was naturalized in 1970, America had been at war with Russia. The moment I became an American citizen, I would have automatically been at war with Russia. I would have had no other options.

This is also true of every person born into the Kingdom of God. The moment you are born into God's Kingdom, you are at war with the kingdom that is at war with your Kingdom. If you truly understand this, it will explain a whole lot of experiences in your life that you never understood before.

What we have outlined, then, is the structure of Satan's kingdom. It is the enemy's goal to expand his kingdom until he has total control of this present world system. To attain that goal, Satan has a plan that he is actively implementing throughout the world today.

16

Satan's Program for the Close of the Age

We have observed that God has a program for the close of this age, including specific goals, tactics and stages. In the same way, we will see in the following chapters that Satan also has a program with goals and strategies designed to accomplish that program. We would do well to know the specifics of the enemy's goals and plans.

As we have seen, Satan has a rival kingdom in the heavenlies composed of spiritual beings without bodies. Their sole purpose under Satan's direction is to oppose and resist God, His people and His purposes. It is against these spiritual beings that we must wrestle and contend.

Many Christians do not realize that Satan has such a program; this ignorance does not negate the fact that it is true. Satan is steadily working toward specific objectives. Unfortunately, we are liable to be deceived or to be ineffective in our warfare against him unless we have some idea of what he is seeking to achieve and the methods he is using.

As we have seen, Satan, by his name, is the resister. He is the one who opposes the purposes and the people of God. We can understand, therefore, that whatever God seeks to do of good, Satan will oppose it with his purposes of evil. Also, as we will soon see in our study, Satan is essentially a counterfeiter. He takes the genuine good that God has provided and seeks to substitute something that is evil but has the outward appearance of good.

Sons of Disobedience

Let's look again at Ephesians 2:2–3. The apostle Paul is writing to believers in Christ, speaking about their former lives.

> In which you once walked according to the course of this world, according to the prince of the power of the air, the spirit who now works in the sons of disobedience, among whom also we all once conducted ourselves in the lusts of our flesh, fulfilling the desires of the flesh and of the mind, and were by nature children of wrath, just as the others.

In this passage, Paul says that as far as the unconverted and unregenerated are concerned, Satan is their ruler. He is the ruler of the realm of authority that we previously defined as "the air." Earlier we saw that this was precisely the realm of authority that God originally committed to Adam. Adam had divine authority over all the earth. When Adam fell by becoming disloyal and turning to Satan, he handed over the whole realm of his authority.

In this way, Satan became the ruler of the realm of the authority of the air, working as a spirit in those humans who are disobedient to God. Satan's rule, however, is valid only over those who are disobedient to God. When an individual turns back to God in true repentance, faith and submission, then Satan's legal claim and dominion over that one is terminated. Even so, Satan is still the ruler over the children of disobedience, the rebellious and all who are unregenerate. All persons who refuse to believe and submit to God have a king over them. This "king" is identified in Job 41 as Leviathan, the king over all the children of pride. Pride, rebellion and stubbornness give Satan his legal claim and his dominion over this group of persons.

Even though Satan is a ruler in this world today, he does not have everything exactly the way he wants it. He has access to the human race through its disobedience to God, but he does not have the human race totally under his command. From my understanding of Scripture, the angels that joined with him in rebellion against God are under Satan's control and must do what he demands. It is obvious, however, that although Satan has a measure of control over sinners and world systems, his dominion is not absolute.

The Role of the Spirit

As we approach the end of the age, I believe Satan has two primary goals toward which he is working: first, to gain total political control on earth through human political governments; and, second, to receive the worship of the entire world for himself. These are objectives toward which Satan has been working for all of history. As we approach the close of this age, his objectives are coming nearer to fulfillment, just has we have seen that God's plan for the close of the age is also nearing fulfillment.

I believe, with certain limitations, that God is going to allow Satan a brief opportunity to fulfill these two objectives as part of God's judgment on the world for rejecting Christ and His Kingdom. It is very important to understand, however, that a great restraining force in the world prevents Satan from the ultimate achievement of his ambitions. That restraining force is the Spirit of God. It is the Spirit who is moving hearts toward repentance, as well as faith in God, in His Word and in Jesus Christ. Wherever men or women are turned back to God in repentance and submission, Satan's dominion over them terminates. As long as the Spirit of God is at work in the world, Satan's dominion will never fully become what he has envisioned.

Many people do not realize that the human race left to itself will remain in rebellion and sin. Humans will never turn to God apart from the Spirit of God, which is the Spirit of grace. There is nothing in unregenerate, fallen, rebellious humanity that will ever prompt them to turn to God unless they are first moved by the Holy Spirit. This is a great truth of Scripture that many people do not understand, but much that is basic in the Gospel rests on this fact. We are dependent upon the Spirit of God for our initial turning to God.

We see a picture in Psalm 14:1–3 of what is working in the heart of mankind apart from the Spirit of God.

> The fool has said in his heart, "There is no God." They are corrupt, they have done abominable works, there is none who does good. The LORD looks down from heaven upon the children of men, to see if there are any who understand, who seek God. They have all turned aside, they have together become corrupt; there is none who does good, no, not one.

Without the Spirit of God at work, humanity does not understand, seek God or do good. We often deceive ourselves, imagining that there was something good in us that caused us to turn to God and receive Jesus Christ. For many years, I said of myself, "I always had a longing in my heart for the truth." In a way I was patting myself on the back. Then one day, God spoke to me out of Scripture by the Holy Spirit: "Don't pride yourself on that, because if My Spirit hadn't put love for the truth in you, it would never have been there."

Now that we are aware that Satan has a program for the close of the age—one that can be altered by the Spirit of God—let's dig in further. In our next chapter we will make ourselves aware of some of Satan's tactics in the world to try to accomplish his goals.

17

Looking for a Man

In order to accomplish his plan for the end of the age, Satan is looking for a man through whom he can fulfill his objectives. To begin to understand this, we look first at the part of Jesus' temptation in the wilderness by Satan that deals with earthly kingdoms and rule.

> Then the devil, taking Him up on a high mountain, showed Him all the kingdoms of the world in a moment of time. And the devil said to Him, "All this authority I will give You, and their glory; for this has been delivered to me, and I give it to whomever I wish. Therefore, if You will worship before me, all will be Yours." And Jesus answered and said to him, "Get behind Me, Satan! For it is written, 'You shall worship the LORD your God, and Him only you shall serve.'"
>
> Luke 4:5–8

Satan's supreme objective is to be worshiped by the whole earth. His strategy is to use a man to gain political control over the entire earth in order that this man may convince the whole earth to worship Satan. Satan said to Jesus, "If You will worship me, then I will give you the power to be the world ruler."

Satan knew what would happen if he gave Jesus this power. The world would acknowledge Jesus, yet they would actually be acknowledging Satan—because Satan was the one who gave Jesus that power. In worshiping Jesus, therefore, they would be worshiping Satan. But Jesus said, "Satan, I will not do it, because there's only one whom we may worship. That is the Lord God." Jesus refused, but Satan is still looking for a man whom he can use as an alternative to Jesus. He is looking for a man whom the world will worship as a messiah.

Christ or Antichrist?

I believe that everywhere Christ is proclaimed, the devil will follow with his alternative, which is an antichrist. Thus, the whole race is continually faced with a choice: Christ or antichrist? The first time this choice was put before the human race was when Jesus stood before Pontius Pilate, and Pilate gave people the choice between releasing Jesus or releasing Barabbas. We all know which choice was made.

I believe this was the first time the spirit of antichrist was manifested in human history. The force of that spirit was sufficient to cause the Jews to reject the true Christ and choose an evil, godless, cunning and violent man. Barabbas is one of the many types in Scripture of an antichrist. As we will see later, the Passover lamb in the Old Testament is a picture—or type—of Christ, the Lamb of God in the New Testament. In the case of this choice offered to people for either Jesus or Barabbas, we see a clear picture of the Antichrist who will be fully revealed in the future.

This will also be the pattern for the close of this age. God will again present the human race with the choice. Whom do you want: the true Christ or the false christ? But before that happens, the true Christ will be preached in all nations for a witness to the whole world with signs following and with the demonstration of the Holy Spirit. Then Satan will be permitted to follow afterward with his Antichrist—and the world will be forced to make a clear-cut decision. The Messiah or Barabbas? There was no third alternative then, and at the close of this age there will be no third alternative. This is the valley of decision spoken about in Joel 3:14: "Multitudes, multitudes in the valley of decision!"

Israel always has the first opportunity when it comes to God's dealings. The Gospel was given to the Jew first and also to the Gentile (see Romans 1:16). Israel had the choice first. Now, all nations will have the choice at the close of this age: "Whom do you want? Jesus or Barabbas?"

An Enticing Choice

Let's look now at Satan's alternatives. Since Jesus, the true Christ, would not make a bargain, the devil is looking for another man of outstanding ability and personality. The enemy will need a man who the world would say has "charisma." This word *charisma*, which has become a popular word in our culture, comes from the Greek word for "grace" or "favor." There is a charisma that comes from the Holy Spirit. On the other hand, there is a kind of charisma that comes from another spirit. The difference is not always easy to distinguish.

Because Satan cannot use just any man for this position, he must find a man of brilliant personality, appearance, intelligence and force of character. Jesus would have been the ideal choice, but He refused to make the bargain with the devil.

"The Beast" is one of the titles of the Antichrist as he is depicted in Revelation:

> Now the beast which I saw was like a leopard, his feet were like the feet of a bear, and his mouth like the mouth of a lion. The dragon [who is the devil] gave him his power, his throne, and great authority. And I saw one of his heads as if it had been mortally wounded, and his deadly wound was healed. And all the world marveled and followed the beast. So they worshiped the dragon who gave authority to the beast; and they worshiped the beast, saying, "Who is like the beast? Who is able to make war with him?"
>
> Revelation 13:2–4

Apparently the Antichrist will be raised from the dead by a miracle, and this will cause the world to marvel and follow him. As unusual as this might sound, how would Americans have received John F. Kennedy if he had been brought back from the dead? He would have had the whole nation at his feet. This is no criticism of the former president, but it is an illustration of the impact such an event would have upon a nation.

No one will be able to make war against the Beast, because he will have all governments and all of their military might under his control. He will have secret police and intelligence services that no one can resist, because Ezekiel 28:3 says that he will be wiser than Daniel and that no secret can be hidden from him. He will have supernatural understanding and wisdom imparted by Satan.

Satan's supreme objective is first to raise up his representative who will rule all nations in opposition to the true

Christ—and then, through the Antichrist, to receive the worship of the world. In worshiping the Antichrist, the world will actually be worshiping Satan, who gave him his power.

Satan's Tactics

In working toward this end of receiving the world's worship, Satan uses two primary tactics. First, he will use direct intervention by spiritual agents from his kingdom. Second, he will empower the outworking of sin's corruption in the human heart, producing progressive moral and ethical decline. Some people would lead us to believe that the world is getting better and better. This can never be true where sin is at work. Conditions will not get better and better. Rather, they will continue to become worse and worse unless God intervenes by His grace.

In the twentieth century, the world witnessed two of the most cruel, wicked, ruthless, destructive rulers that human history has ever recorded: Adolph Hitler and Josef Stalin. Each of them was directly responsible for the brutal killing of tens of millions of human beings. I do not believe there has been anything in human history that parallels the activities of those two men. Furthermore, recent history continues to produce similar men: Pol Pot, Saddam Hussein and the leaders of North Korea to name just a few. The human race is not getting better. Only the corruption of humanity could make it possible to accept rulers like Stalin and Hitler.

Not only is Satan continually raising up evil men, a second part of his strategy is the direct, supernatural intervention of evil spirits. These two strategies are cooperating to produce a corrupt culture and the one ruler whom Satan desires.

18

The Days of Noah

There are two patterns of corrupt society in the Old Testament, each of which illuminates several truths concerning this culminating project of Satan. The first, which will be the subject of this chapter, is from the days of Noah. The second pattern is from the days of Ahab, King of Israel, and it will be the focus of our next chapter.

Beginning with the example of the days of Noah, we see the pattern unfolding.

> Now it came to pass, when men began to multiply on the face of the earth, and daughters were born to them, that the sons of God saw the daughters of men, that they were beautiful; and they took wives for themselves of all whom they chose.
>
> Genesis 6:1–2

Some may disagree, but I firmly believe that the phrase *sons of God* in this passage refers to fallen angels. These were not the loyal angels of God, but angels who joined Lucifer in rebellion against God. At some point they came down from the angelic heavenlies and cohabited with human women.

Unholy Interaction

It is interesting that numerous ancient myths and various records of human races around the world preserve these postulations; they are not recorded in the Scriptures only. Most of the heroes (whom you could call "men of renown") in Greek and Roman mythology had their origins from a god having sexual relations with a human woman, as Zeus did with Leda in Greek mythology.

I would not believe these things if they were merely ancient myths. The Bible, however, presents the same picture.

> There were giants [Hebrew, Nephilim or fallen ones] on the earth in those days, and also afterward, when the sons of God came in to the daughters of men and they bore children to them. Those were the mighty men who were of old, men of renown.
>
> Genesis 6:4

In the past—and presently as well—there was direct intervention from the spiritual realm by Satan's representatives in the human race. This interaction was the root cause of all the corruption that we mention in this chapter, ultimately culminating in God's judgment through the universal flood. The origin of this corruption was intervention from Satan's realm. The fact that it was supernatural intervention that triggered the process of corruption explains why it developed so quickly.

Some people object to this theory, saying that angels do not marry. They cite Jesus' statement in Mark 12:25. Note, however, Jesus said that the angels *in heaven* do not marry. Elsewhere in Scripture there are records of these fallen angels leaving their own realm and changing their appearance. In the course of my ministry, I have had personal contact with at least three cases of women who have told me that demons have sought to have sexual intercourse with them.

There are two comparative passages in the New Testament. The first is 1 Peter 3:19–20: "By whom also He [Jesus] went and preached to the spirits in prison [Hades, the place of the dead], who formerly were disobedient, when once the Divine longsuffering waited in the days of Noah."

There were spirits imprisoned in Hades whom God had imprisoned there for a specific purpose. Greek mythology is full of references to a place called Tartarus. Tartarus is a place of special imprisonment that is as far below Hades as Hades is below the surface of the earth. In the Greek New Testament, this word is translated "hell" (see 2 Peter 2:4) and is used in reference to these rebellious angels. The Bible and mythology in this respect are in agreement.

A particular group of angels was imprisoned in this special place, even below the regular prison in Hades. Evidently, Jesus descended into this realm in the period between His death and resurrection. He did not preach the Gospel to them, but He made some sort of proclamation to them.

We find a similar reference in Jude 6–7:

> And the angels who did not keep their proper domain [did not stay in the heavenlies], but left their own abode, He has reserved in everlasting chains under darkness for the judgment of the great day; as Sodom and Gomorrah, and the cities around them in a similar manner to these, having given themselves over to sexual immorality and gone after strange flesh, are set forth as an example, suffering the vengeance of eternal fire.

It seems clear to me that just as homosexuality is "strange flesh" as it applies within the human race, so is this reference to angels going outside the bounds of their natural being. They were going after "strange flesh" in cohabiting with human women.

There is no need to dwell on this rather unsavory topic. It is helpful, however, to observe that the Bible presents an absolutely clear, consistent picture. Scripture confirms that satanic, supernatural intervention was the source of the final avalanche of moral decline that precipitated the flood.

Continual Evil

We now take a more in-depth look at the moral decline that was initiated by this supernatural intervention, focusing on three verses in Genesis 6.

> Then the LORD saw that the wickedness of man was great in the earth, and that every intent [every imagination, KJV] of the thoughts of his heart was only evil continually (verse 5).

> (The point of moral decline cited here is *evil imaginations*.)

> The earth also was corrupt before God, and the earth was filled with violence (verse 11).

> (The point of moral decline cited here is *violence*.)

> So God looked upon the earth, and indeed it was corrupt; for all flesh had corrupted their way on the earth (verse 12).

> (The point of moral decline cited here is *corruption*.)

I understand *corruption* to mean sexual corruption and perversion. These, then, were the three main features of human degeneration prior to the flood: evil imaginations, violence, and sexual corruption and perversion. Looking at modern America and much of the West, most of these points of moral decline are manifesting and increasing in our world today. I have pointed out that the Holy Spirit is the restraining influence that prevents Satan from taking complete control. The Spirit is able to be that restraining force as long as He can operate in the human heart to create repentance and faith in Jesus Christ.

Channels of Righteousness

I want to point out that the Holy Spirit must have a channel through whom to work. The channel at that time was Noah and his family. When Noah and his family were withdrawn, God's Spirit was withdrawn along with them. There was a period of seven days when Satan had total control, and then came the final judgment.

There is something worthy of note in Genesis 7:1: "Then the Lord said to Noah, 'Come into the ark, you and all your household, because I have seen that you are righteous before Me in this generation.'"

It was the righteousness of Noah that saved his family. God did not say, "I've seen that you and your family are righteous." Rather, He allowed Noah's family in because *Noah* was righteous. Acts 16:31 says, "Believe on the Lord Jesus Christ, and you will be saved, you and your household." This pattern goes all through the Bible. Clearly, we have the right to believe for the salvation of our households. I do not mean that our families will be saved without faith in Jesus Christ, but we have a right to believe that they will come to have faith in Jesus Christ. This is not to imply that Noah's family were unbelievers, but they became believers because of God's grace working in Noah.

Seven Days

Returning to the narrative we read:

> For after seven more days I [God] will cause it to rain on the earth forty days and forty nights, and I will destroy from the face of the earth all living things that I have made. . . . So Noah, with his sons, his wife, and his sons' wives, went into the ark because of the waters of the flood. . . . And it came to pass after seven days that the waters of the flood were on the earth.
>
> Genesis 7:4, 7, 10

There was a period of seven days before the flood when Noah and his family were shut inside the ark, and Scripture says God shut the door. During those seven days, in a certain sense, the human race was given over to Satan because the Spirit of God had moved into the ark with Noah and his family.

Jesus indicates that Noah's experience is a pattern for conditions at the close of this age. Jesus declared, "As it was in the days of Noah, so it will be also in the days of the Son of Man" (Luke 17:26). These basic patterns will be reproduced at the close of this age, including direct, satanic supernatural intervention by demonic spirits. The patterns will also include ever-increasing corruption, lawlessness, violence and immorality. But as we will see in the chapters ahead, God is going to have a people who will be a restraining influence on the basis of grace and righteousness.

When God withdraws those people, however, the influence of the Spirit of God will be withdrawn. For a period of time the human race will, in a certain sense, be handed over to Satan. Following that period will come the final judgment. I am not asking anybody to believe what I am saying. For me, however, I see this pattern in Scripture, and I believe it to be true.

19

The Pattern of Ahab

Along with the experience of Noah and his family discussed in our previous chapter, I believe there is also a pattern for the closing of the age from the days of King Ahab. Ahab was a king of Israel who was exceedingly wicked. In the days of Ahab's reign, Israel was the northern kingdom—which did not include the southern kingdom, Judah.

Certain features of Ahab's wickedness and the dark forces at work in his kingdom make this period in Israel's history a type, or a pattern, for the close of this age. When we look at Israel in Ahab's day, we find some of the same forces at work in our day: degeneration of human character and satanic supernatural intervention.

Weak and Childish

Let's look at the primary individuals involved.

In the thirty-eighth year of Asa king of Judah, Ahab the son of Omri became king over Israel; and Ahab the son of Omri reigned over Israel in Samaria twenty-two years. Now Ahab the son of Omri did evil in the sight of the LORD, more than all who were before him. And it came to pass, as though it had been a trivial thing for him to walk in the sins of Jeroboam the son of Nebat, that he took as wife Jezebel the daughter of Ethbaal, king of the Sidonians; and he went and served Baal and worshiped him. Then he set up an altar for Baal in the temple of Baal, which he had built in Samaria. And Ahab made a wooden image. Ahab did more to provoke the LORD God of Israel to anger than all the kings of Israel who were before him.

1 Kings 16:29–33

Ahab was stubborn and wicked. But he also had a weak character and, in a certain way, a childish character. When Ahab could not get Naboth's vineyard, he went home and cried on his bed until his wife, Jezebel, fixed it for him by plotting the murder of Naboth (see 1 Kings 21:1–16). Ahab had a terribly degenerate character like many monarchs in recent history. Such monarchs may wield tremendous power, yet behave like little children when something does not suit them.

We see a typical brand of person in Ahab: weak, capricious, dishonest, cruel, unstable and unreliable, yet rather clever. His weak character allowed him to be taken over by a dominating, shrewd and scheming wife, which is precisely what happened to him.

In 1 Kings 21:25, Ahab is summed up in a single verse: "There was no one like Ahab who sold himself to do wickedness in the sight of the LORD, because Jezebel his wife stirred him up."

Notice Ahab "sold" himself. He made a bargain with Satan and, in so doing, put himself at the devil's disposal. Ahab is another type of the Antichrist in that he bargained with the devil. Everything presented in Scripture as a type is a picture of reality; the realities of human nature and how the forces of evil work. Ahab selling himself to Satan is a type of the Antichrist, who will give himself to Satan so that he can have the devil's power.

I have ministered to individuals who have made bargains with Satan by praying to him. Some of the most terrible cases of demon possession I have ever encountered were in people who actually made a bargain with the devil. When they bargained with the devil he then regarded them as his property for time and eternity. Getting such persons free of the resulting demonic oppression is a major battle.

Jezebel, Ahab's wife, supported him in his wickedness with satanic supernatural power and demonic worship. In that respect, Jezebel is a type of the false church, which will make an alliance with the Antichrist at the close of this age for a short period of time.

The Evil of Jezebel

It will be enlightening for us to consider Ahab's wife, Jezebel, because she is a type of the Harlot in Revelation 17 and 18. She is the picture of the idolatrous, cruel and wicked false church. We see an initial description of her evil ways in 1 Kings: "For so it was, while Jezebel massacred the prophets of the LORD, that Obadiah had taken one hundred prophets and hidden them, fifty to a cave, and had fed them with bread and water" (1 Kings 18:4).

Jezebel was the persecutor of the Lord's prophets. She killed them ruthlessly. Obadiah said to Elijah: "Was it not reported to my lord what I did when Jezebel killed the prophets of the Lord, how I hid one hundred men of the Lord's prophets, fifty to a cave, and fed them with bread and water?" (verse 13).

Jezebel was out to destroy every true prophet of the Lord, while simultaneously promoting the false prophets of Baal and Asherah. But Elijah sent a message to Ahab: "Now therefore, send and gather all Israel to me on Mount Carmel, the four hundred and fifty prophets of Baal, and the four hundred prophets of Asherah, who eat at Jezebel's table" (1 Kings 18:19).

Jezebel maintained and pampered eight hundred and fifty false prophets—but she killed the prophets of the Lord. This will also be true of the false church that will rise up at the close of this age. It will persecute the true servants of God while promoting false prophets and false christs.

The real source of Jezebel's power is revealed in 2 Kings 9:22, the passage cited below. Before examining this verse, we need to have the background. At this point, Ahab had been killed and Joram, who was Jezebel's son, had become king of Israel. Jehu, however, had been anointed as king of Israel by Elijah at the Lord's command (see 1 Kings 19:16). In the setting of this verse, Jehu has encountered Joram, and Joram is asking Jehu if he comes in peace. "Now it happened, when Joram saw Jehu, that he said, 'Is it peace, Jehu?' So he [Jehu] answered, 'What peace, as long as the harlotries of your mother Jezebel and her witchcraft are so many?'"

Jezebel was a practicing witch—she had direct interaction with satanic supernatural power. The witchcraft of Jezebel plus the corruption and wickedness of Ahab's character produced a situation in which the forces of Satan had practically taken over the entire kingdom of Israel.

God's Answer

At this point, God's answer to this situation was a new type of ministry: the ministry of Elijah. Elijah's ministry represented God's response to the alliance of political power and satanic supernatural power represented by Ahab and Jezebel. The following verses help us understand what God had in mind.

> And Elijah the Tishbite, of the inhabitants of Gilead, said to Ahab, "As the LORD God of Israel lives, before whom I stand, there shall not be dew nor rain these years, except at my word." . . . And it came to pass after many days that the word of the LORD came to Elijah, in the third year, saying, "Go, present yourself to Ahab, and I will send rain on the earth."
>
> 1 Kings 17:1; 18:1

Elijah was God's answer to the situation. By God's command, He brought judgment against the forces of Satan working to dominate Israel through the political, demonic alliance of Ahab and Jezebel.

Let us not be deceived. The final battle is not going to be fought on the plane of human reasoning and argument. It is going to be fought on a supernatural plane. When the power of Jezebel's prophets had almost taken over the land, God sent Elijah, a prophet who would call down fire from heaven.

We read in Scripture the account of the confrontation that took place between Elijah and the prophets of Baal. The false prophets agreed, the true prophets agreed, the king agreed and the people agreed: "The God who answers by fire, He is God" (1 Kings 18:24). In other words, let's have a demonstration. Not just words; let's see it done. That is the message to the world today and it is the message that the Church must accept. We cannot sidestep this challenge.

We are obligated to produce the evidence of God's superior power, because Satan's servants are demonstrating their power already.

At the close of this age—when the Beast and the false church rise up—the situation will again require a similar ministry sent by God. As Malachi 4:5 says, "Behold, I [God speaking to His people] will send you Elijah the prophet before the coming of the great and dreadful day of the LORD."

Elijah's ministry is specifically related to a situation where political power is usurped and then abetted by satanic spiritual power in an attempt to destroy God's people and to overthrow God's Kingdom. That is Satan's program for the close of this age.

20

The Rise of False Prophets

As we have seen from the previous two chapters, Noah's day and Ahab are types of approaching events in this age. But there are also prophetic Scriptures that foresee these situations coming. In speaking about the end times, Jesus gives a prophetic outline of the spiritual and political trends that will manifest themselves. In this sermon He tells us two facts about false prophets and false christs. First, He says, "Many false prophets will rise up and deceive many" (Matthew 24:11). Then He restates it: "False christs and false prophets will rise and show great signs and wonders to deceive, if possible, even the elect" (verse 24).

At the close of the age there will be false prophets and false christs with supernatural power. Further, those who are not rooted in Christ and do not know the power of God and the truth of the Word of God will be deceived. Some people are naive enough to believe that all supernatural power comes from God. This is not true. There are two sources of supernatural power: God on the one hand and Satan on the other. I do not believe there is a third source. Jesus warned us that at the close of this age there will be supernatural satanic power turned loose against the human race with one supreme objective: *to deceive*.

Evil Forces at Work

As we examine other parts of the New Testament, this truth is confirmed. Paul makes a parallel statement: "Now the Spirit expressly says that in latter times [the close of the age] some will depart from the faith, giving heed to deceiving spirits and doctrines of demons" (1 Timothy 4:1).

"The faith" mentioned in this passage is Christianity. It is not just any faith—it is *the* faith. The people about whom Paul is writing have been in the faith. He warns, however, that they will depart from the faith under the influence of seducing, satanic spirits who deceive them by false teaching.

In Paul's letter to Timothy, we see a further picture of the same forces at work: "But evil men and impostors will grow worse and worse, deceiving and being deceived" (2 Timothy 3:13). Where the NKJV says *impostors*, the standard Greek word is for a magician or an enchanter. This is not merely any type of deceiver. It is a person who deliberately cultivates satanic supernatural power. It is a magician who is just like a witch, a wizard, a fortuneteller or a clairvoyant. Such people operate not in their own natural ability and understanding, but by supernatural power and revelation that has a satanic origin. These evil persons of corrupted human nature, who are satanically inspired servants of Satan, will grow worse and worse—deceiving and being deceived.

There is no one as deceptive as the person who is deceived. Sometimes we marvel how a person can tell us enormous lies and ask us to believe such things. The answer is, that person is deceived. He or she really believes what he or she is saying. Those who are deceived are the most deceptive of all people.

I do not know if what I am about to say is correct, but I can believe it. I was once told that a lie detector will detect the reaction of a person who is knowingly telling a lie. It will not, however, detect a pathological liar who believes what he is saying is true, because he has no reaction the lie detector can register. He does not even know he is telling a lie because he is deceived and believes he is telling the truth. I believe in many such cases it really is not the person speaking. It is a spirit who is telling the lie through him.

These people to whom Paul is referring are the really dangerous people. It is not the ones who are deliberately deceiving, telling you what they know is false. Rather, it is the ones who are so totally deceived that they believe the lies they are telling you.

Open Conflict

Just as in the day of Ahab and Elijah, we are going to face an open confrontation of supernatural power in the end times. If we glance back a few verses in 2 Timothy 3, we see why it makes sense to translate *impostors* as "magicians" in verse 13.

> Now as Jannes and Jambres [magicians in the court of Pharaoh] withstood Moses, so do these also resist the truth: men of corrupt minds, reprobate concerning the faith. But they shall proceed no further: for their folly shall be manifest unto all men, as theirs [Jannes' and Jambres'] also was.
>
> Verses 8–9 KJV

130

The reprobates cited in these verses are those who have known the faith and departed from it. A *reprobate* means "one who is rejected." These Scriptures indicate that at the close of this age there is going to be an open conflict between the supernatural power of the Holy Spirit and the servants of God on the one hand, and the satanic power of magicians, wizards, enchanters, clairvoyants and mediums on the other hand. In the end, the servants of Satan are going to be put to an open shame. Their folly will be made manifest to all.

A Supernatural Contest

The Church, if operating only in the natural realm, will not be able to keep up or prevail. In this battle, which is going to be in the supernatural, the Church must operate as well on a supernatural level. If you read carefully the account in Exodus of the clash between Moses and the magicians of Egypt, you see that the magicians had supernatural powers.

> So Moses and Aaron went in to Pharaoh, and they did so, just as the LORD commanded. And Aaron cast down his rod before Pharaoh and before his servants, and it became a serpent. But Pharaoh also called the wise men and the sorcerers; so the magicians of Egypt, they also did in like manner with their enchantments. For every man threw down his rod, and they became serpents. But Aaron's rod swallowed up their rods.
>
> Exodus 7:10–12

Please notice that Aaron's rod swallowed up the rods of the magicians. The supernatural power of God will always ultimately triumph over the power of Satan.

131

Still, I would imagine that Pharaoh said to Moses, "My magicians can do the same thing Aaron can do. Why should I believe you have a message from God that I should listen to?" The tests of supernatural power continued.

> Then the LORD spoke to Moses, "Say to Aaron, 'Take your rod and stretch out your hand over the waters of Egypt, over their streams, over their rivers, over their ponds, and over all their pools of water, that they may become blood. And there shall be blood throughout all the land of Egypt, both in buckets of wood and pitchers of stone.'" And Moses and Aaron did so, just as the LORD commanded. So he lifted up the rod and struck the waters that were in the river, in the sight of Pharaoh and in the sight of his servants. And all the waters that were in the river were turned to blood. . . . Then the magicians of Egypt did so with their enchantments.
>
> Exodus 7:19–20, 22

The Egyptian magicians could also turn water into blood. Once again, Pharaoh might have said, "Moses, why should I believe you have a message for me? My magicians can do the same."

The next confrontation had to do with frogs.

> Then the LORD spoke to Moses, "Say to Aaron, 'Stretch out your hand with your rod over the streams, over the rivers, and over the ponds, and cause frogs to come up on the land of Egypt.'" So Aaron stretched out his hand over the waters of Egypt, and the frogs came up and covered the land of Egypt. And the magicians did so with their enchantments, and brought up frogs on the land of Egypt.
>
> Exodus 8:5–7

Again Pharaoh would have said, "I don't have to listen to you. My magicians can do the same."

The next time, however, was where the difference manifested.

> So the LORD said to Moses, "Say to Aaron, 'Stretch out your rod, and strike the dust of the land, so that it may become lice throughout all the land of Egypt.'" And they did so. For Aaron stretched out his hand with his rod and struck the dust of the earth, and it became lice on man and beast. All the dust of the land became lice throughout all the land of Egypt. Now the magicians so worked with their enchantments to bring forth lice, but they could not. So there were lice on man and beast. Then the magicians said to Pharaoh, "This is the finger of God."
>
> Exodus 8:16–19

At least the Egyptian magicians were realistic. They knew they were witnessing supernatural power on a higher level than their magic could achieve. By the same token, they were not going to bow to a power that was less powerful than what they had. This is the nature of the spiritual conflict we will face in the end times.

The Generation We Face

The New Testament predicts the increase of lawlessness and moral decline, exactly as it was in the days before Noah's flood. In Jesus' sermon about the close of the age, He says, "Because lawlessness will abound, the love of many will grow cold" (Matthew 24:12).

The Greek translation of this phrase reads, "The love of the majority will grow cold." The word for *love* is *agape*, the word that is used only for God's love and the love of God's people. In other words, the love of most of God's people will grow cold because of an atmosphere of abounding lawlessness and immorality all around.

Second Timothy 3 is one of the key chapters in relation to the end times. It presents us with the picture of complete moral and ethical breakdown as the end approaches.

> But know this, that in the last days perilous times will come: For men will be lovers of themselves, lovers of money, boasters, proud, blasphemers, disobedient to parents, unthankful, unholy, unloving, unforgiving, slanderers, without self-control, brutal, despisers of good, traitors, headstrong, haughty, lovers of pleasure rather than lovers of God, having a form of godliness but denying its power. And from such people turn away!
>
> 2 Timothy 3:1–5

The passage begins and ends with love—but the wrong kind of love: in the beginning "lovers of themselves" and "lovers of money" and in the ending "lovers of pleasure." I would invite you to take a close look at this generation in the world today. Ask yourself, "Has there ever been a generation that was more taken up with love of self, love of money and love of pleasure than the present generation?"

Then, if you look at all the other moral failures Paul lists here, you will find that almost every one of them is conspicuous in our generation. If the human race had not degenerated to this degree, neither Hitler nor Stalin could ever have gained control. Why? Because men and women would have never done the wicked acts Hitler and Stalin asked them to do.

Verse 5 says that this culture has "a form of godliness." Even with all this wickedness, moral corruption and ethical decline, the people will still claim to be religious. It is hard to believe that, isn't it? Yet in our day those people could be any denomination of Christianity. In fact, I believe the Lord has shown me that in many cases, religious claims are the driving force of their error. It was Jezebel's religion that made Ahab so wicked.

At the end of the age, that is again how it will be: false religion that not only covers up but also promotes the moral and ethical decline. It is not an accident that false religion and moral decline are joined together. They represent a cause-and-effect relationship. Our society continues to move rapidly in that direction.

No Compromise

Notice one other factor. Paul includes a warning: "From such, turn away." If you are around people in your church circle of friends who answer to this description, the Bible urges you to turn away and disassociate yourself.

In fact, a great deal is said in 2 Timothy about disassociating yourself from evil.

> Nevertheless the solid foundation of God stands, having this seal: "The Lord knows those who are His," and, "Let everyone who names the name of Christ depart from iniquity." But in a great house there are not only vessels of gold and silver, but also of wood and clay, some for honor and some for dishonor.
>
> 2 Timothy 2:19–20

There are two seals of the true Christian: first, the inward knowledge that God knows us as His children; and, second, an outward life of holiness. Paul says in this verse that anyone who names the name of Christ is obligated to depart from iniquity. The question is whether we wish to be a vessel for honor or a vessel for dishonor. If we want to be vessels for honor, we must heed the next verses.

Therefore if anyone cleanses himself from the latter, he will be a vessel for honor, sanctified and useful for the Master, prepared for every good work. Flee also youthful lusts; but pursue righteousness, faith, love, peace with those who call on the Lord out of a pure heart.

Verses 21–22

It matters with whom you associate. If you want to follow righteousness, faith, peace and charity, you must remain with those who call on the Lord out of a pure heart. Clearly, there is coming a separation of paths between the godly and the godless: "For the time is at hand. He who is unjust, let him be unjust still; he who is filthy, let him be filthy still; he who is righteous, let him be righteous still; he who is holy, let him be holy still" (Revelation 22:10–11).

We must go one way or the other—compromise is not an option. God is forcing the entire human race into the valley of decision. No one will come out of that valley without making a decision.

In these sections we have begun to understand Satan's agenda for the end times. As Satan advances his agenda, what is the Church of Jesus Christ called to do? As we mentioned earlier, part of God's purpose for His people is to engage actively in the restraining and casting down of Satan's kingdom. Toward that end Scripture reveals that God has committed to His Church two specific responsibilities. The first is to restrain Satan's purposes on the earth until God's work of grace has been completed. The second is to cast down Satan's kingdom from the heavenlies.

21

The Church's Responsibility

As we turn to the responsibilities facing us as Christians in the end times, let's take a few moments to recap what we have learned. We have seen that God has three major objectives on earth for the Church. The first is to reap the earth's last great harvest of souls, initiating an outpouring of God's Spirit at the close of this age. In fact, Jesus said, "The harvest *is* the end of the age" (Matthew 13:39, emphasis added).

Secondly, the Church is to prepare herself as a Bride for Christ, who is the Bridegroom.

Thirdly, the Church is to be an instrument of restraining and casting down Satan and his kingdom, which will be the subject of the next few chapters.

We have also seen that Satan has his own specific objectives for the close of this age. The first goal is to gain complete political control through a man who is portrayed in Scripture under the title of *Antichrist*.

Secondly, Satan's goal through this man is to receive universal worship—the devil's ultimate objective since his fall.

Through this political ruler whom he plans to raise up at the close of this age, Satan will—for a short period of time—receive almost universal worship on earth.

In opposition to these two purposes of Satan, Christ has committed to His Church two special responsibilities. The first is *to restrain Satan's purposes on earth* until God's purposes of grace have been fulfilled. God will not totally prevent Satan from accomplishing his purposes, and will actually permit him to succeed for a short period. It is the responsibility of the disciples of Christ, the true Church, to restrain the full accomplishment of Satan's purposes until God's purposes of grace have been fulfilled.

The second responsibility that Christ has committed to His followers is *to cast down Satan's kingdom from the heavenlies.* Though this fact is clearly stated in Scripture, I have met very few Christians who understand this. In fact, it came as a surprise to me when I first saw it in Scripture.

These are the two special powers that Christ has committed to us as His disciples. The first is the power of believers to restrain Satan's activities. The second is the power of believers to cast down Satan's kingdom.

Salt of the Earth

In this chapter and the ones that follow we will consider the power of believers to restrain Satan. In His Sermon on the Mount, Jesus gives us the essence of this truth: "You are the salt of the earth; but if the salt loses its flavor, how shall it be seasoned? It is then good for nothing but to be thrown out and trampled underfoot by men" (Matthew 5:13).

Salt has two important attributes—and both relate to our function as believers in the earth today. First, salt adds flavor to food. Salt brings out the taste and enhances the goodness in certain foods, making them pleasing to the palate. Second, salt has the ability to restrain the processes of corruption and is used as a preservative. Let's consider each of these functions in some detail.

Salt imparts flavor to make something acceptable that otherwise would not be tolerable. Jesus said we are the "salt of the earth." We are here, therefore, to give flavor to the earth—to make the earth acceptable to God. Otherwise, without our presence, it would not be acceptable before God. In other words, as long as we are here, we cause God—by our presence—to look down upon the earth and deal with it in grace, mercy and favor rather than in wrath and final judgment. It is our presence that keeps back the final judgment and causes God to offer mercy and grace to the earth as a whole.

Salt is not applied in large blobs or spoonfuls. It is sprinkled just a few grains at a time. But each little grain has its particular function and purpose: to give flavor to that particular area where it is sprinkled. That is how we, as believers, are ordained to be in the earth. Each one of us should be functioning as a grain of salt, creating an atmosphere in our own particular area that causes God to look with favor and mercy—not merely upon us, but on the people who are around us. I think many Christians have not realized this. You and I are responsible for the situation in which we live, and we are responsible for the atmosphere around us.

Salt in Sodom

Let's look at some illustrations of this principle in which we see true believers being the "salt of the earth." In each instance, the presence of believers caused God to view the situation or the group of people involved with mercy and favor. If those believers had been absent, God would have withdrawn His mercy and the only option left would have been His wrath and judgment.

We will look first at God's dealing with Sodom in Genesis 18. The Lord had visited Abraham and told him He was on a journey to see the wickedness of Sodom prior to bringing judgment upon the city. Do you remember who lived in Sodom? It was Abraham's nephew, Lot. Abraham, therefore, had a very special reason for being concerned. As a result, Abraham decided that he would talk to the Lord about His intentions to bring judgment upon Sodom.

> And Abraham came near [to the Lord] and said, "Would You also destroy the righteous with the wicked? Suppose there were fifty righteous within the city; would You also destroy the place and not spare it for the fifty righteous that were in it? Far be it from You to do such a thing as this, to slay the righteous with the wicked, so that the righteous should be as the wicked; far be it from You! Shall not the Judge of all the earth do right?"
>
> Genesis 18:23–25

Many believers have not grasped the truth that was clear to Abraham: God would never deal with the righteous in the same way He did with the wicked. It is altogether out of the question that God, who is a just God, would ever place His judgments for wickedness upon the righteous. Abraham saw this clearly.

If any judgment at any time descends upon the wicked, it should not come near us if we are believers in Jesus Christ. It should not touch those of us who have been made righteous by faith in Jesus, nor should it bring fear over us. It is alien to the justice of God to deal with the righteous as with the wicked.

So Abraham said, "If there are only fifty righteous people in Sodom, wouldn't You spare the city for the sake of fifty righteous?"

God agreed, "If I find in Sodom fifty righteous within the city, then I will spare all the place for their sakes."

We do not need to read the verses after that to remember that Abraham brought the number down, ten by ten.

"What about forty?"

"Well, all right, I'll spare it for forty."

"What about thirty?"

"Well, I'll spare it for thirty."

"What about twenty?"

"I'll spare it for twenty."

Finally, Abraham said, "I'm just going to talk once more, Lord, just once more. Suppose there were only ten? Would you spare it for the sake of ten?"

The Lord said, "I will not destroy it for the sake of ten."

I do not know how many people lived in Sodom, but I imagine it was a fairly large city. I would also imagine that the proportion regarding Sodom still applies today. Ten righteous men in that city could have caused God to dispel His judgment and withhold His wrath for the whole city.

How would we characterize those ten righteous persons? Had they been there, they would have been the "salt of the earth." They would have been ten little grains of salt that made the whole city acceptable to God so that He would not deal with it in wrath and judgment. This is what it is to be the salt of the earth.

A Focal Point

Elisha the prophet is another example of the influence one person can have. In 2 Kings, we read that Elisha was in the city of Dothan, and the king of Syria had sent an army with many horses and chariots to take Elisha prisoner. On the morning when the army of Syria arrived, Elisha's servant rose early. When he went outside, an awful scene met his eyes.

> And when the servant of the man of God arose early and went out, there was an army, surrounding the city with horses and chariots. And his servant said to him, "Alas, my master! What shall we do?"
>
> So he [Elisha] answered, "Do not fear, for those who are with us are more than those who are with them." And Elisha prayed, and said, "LORD, I pray, open his eyes that he may see." Then the LORD opened the eyes of the young man, and he saw. And behold, the mountain was full of horses and chariots of fire all around Elisha.
>
> 2 Kings 6:15–17

Elisha was one man—yet he was the focal point for all the armies of God protecting God's people. One man can have such a relationship with God that the Lord will have all the forces of heaven watching over him. As a result, all the people around him will be protected as well. If you study the rest of the story, the entire city of Dothan was saved because one person was there who knew God and was in right relationship with Him.

Psalm 106 is a record of God's dealings with Israel from Egypt into the Promised Land. Actually, it is primarily a recollection of Israel's transgressions and backslidings. Beginning with verse 20, the psalm recalls Israel's failure in making the golden calf:

Thus they changed their glory into the image of an ox that eats grass. They forgot God their Savior, who had done great things in Egypt, wondrous works in the land of Ham, awesome things by the Red Sea. Therefore He said that He would destroy them, had not Moses His chosen one stood before Him in the breach, to turn away His wrath, lest He destroy them.

Psalm 106:20–23

If you read the account in Exodus 32, you will find that Moses stood between God and the destruction of the whole nation of Israel. Notice that Moses is called God's chosen one, which is one of the titles indicating the favor of God. God's favor toward Moses could cover a whole nation's transgressions!

Finding One Man

In Ezekiel, we see the opposite side of the picture. It was a time of tremendous backsliding in Israel when God could not find even one man who would stand on behalf of the people and hold back His wrath. Ezekiel 22 ends with God giving an outline of evil that involved every section of the nation: "Son of man, say to her: 'You are a land that is not cleansed or rained on in the day of indignation'" (verse 24). Please notice that it is the latter rain that cleanses the land from God's indignation. When the rain does not fall, then the land is not cleansed.

The Lord then points out the different people involved in this wickedness.

"The conspiracy of her prophets" (verse 25).

"Her priests have violated My law" (verse 26).

"Her princes in her midst are like wolves tearing the
prey" (verse 27).
"Her prophets [are] seeing false visions" (verse 28).
"The people of the land [all the common people]
have . . . mistreated the poor and needy" (verse 29).

The prophets, the priests, the princes and the people have
all turned away in transgression and rebellion against God.
Then the Lord says through the prophet: "So I sought for
a man among them who would make a wall, and stand in
the gap before Me on behalf of the land, that I should not
destroy it; but I found no one. Therefore I have poured out
My indignation on them" (verses 30–31).

Notice the *therefore* at the beginning of the last sentence.
In other words, God was saying, "If I could have found one
man, he could have changed the situation. But there wasn't
even one man who could stand before Me in the gap and
make up the hedge."

Unfortunately, I believe the situation in much of the Christian world today is the same. If God does not find *one or
more persons* who will stand in the gap and make up the
hedge, there is no hope in forestalling the judgment of God.

For One Person's Sake

In the book of Acts in the New Testament we find the apostle
Paul, having been brought to trial and transferred to the
judgment of Caesar, on a ship sailing to Rome. Some distance into the journey, the ship runs into a terrible storm.
For fourteen days and nights they do not see the sun or the
stars—at which point they give up all hope of being saved.
An angel of God, however, comes to the ship in the night

144

and speaks to Paul. Paul then says these words to all who are on the ship: "For there stood by me this night an angel of the God to whom I belong and whom I serve, saying, 'Do not be afraid, Paul; you must be brought before Caesar; and indeed God has granted you all those who sail with you'" (Acts 27:23–24).

There were two positive remarks that Paul was able to say about God: "whose I am" and "whom I serve." If you can say that, you have as much right to all the promises of God as Paul did.

Every single person on the ship would be saved for Paul's sake because he had to get to Rome. Satan can hinder, but he can never prevent the fulfillment of God's program. He may delay it, but God's plan will always go through. The whole of heaven was concerned about getting Paul to Rome!

Luke, who was writing the account, says, "And in all we were two hundred and seventy-six persons on the ship" (Acts 27:37). Not counting Paul, there were 275 persons who were spared destruction because of the presence of Paul. The same principle applies today; the presence of true believers makes the difference!

During World War II when I was a medical orderly in the North African desert, I was part of the Lightfield Ambulance. Our unit was attached to an armored division and we were the only unarmed group among them. One of the challenges of serving in the desert was that when a sandstorm came, you had no idea whether you were going north, south, east or west. Consequently, you could end up not knowing if you were behind your lines or enemy lines.

I remember two occasions when we did not know if we were in front of or behind our own lines. There we were, a small medical unit, wandering about with a few trucks in the desert—a rather pitiful sight. More than once, my fellow soldiers, who were not Christians—and especially one man who was really an ungodly blasphemer—came to me and said, "Corporal Prince, I'm glad you're with us." I knew exactly what they meant: "We feel safer when you're here." I am not boasting when I recall this. I simply believe it should be true of every believer; he or she should make a difference by his or her presence.

I was with that unit in what amounted to continuous action in the desert for two years, and we never lost a man killed during that time. I believe that was for my sake. You may think my words conceited—that is up to you. I simply think it occurred because I was a believer, and this is the inheritance of *every* believer. What really impressed me in these situations was that the unbelievers were more aware of the protection my presence brought than some believers! Maybe the unbelievers were not going to get converted by it, but they knew the protection of God accompanied those who trusted in Him.

Heaven's Representatives

As we close this chapter, let's apply 2 Corinthians 5:20 to sum up the role we play in the world around us: "Now then, we are ambassadors for Christ, as though God were pleading through us: we implore you on Christ's behalf, be reconciled to God.

We, as believers, are ambassadors, heaven's authorized representatives in an alien land. We speak on behalf of heaven's government and have the authority of heaven's armies behind us! It is just like any ambassador who fulfills his or her function in the country where he or she is sent. These ambassadors speak with the authority of their governments, and they have the military resources of their governments behind them. As long as we are in the world, we are messengers of reconciliation. As heaven's representatives, we beseech the world, "Be reconciled to God." We are here in Christ's place as ambassadors of peace.

When a nation proposes to declare war on another nation, the last official act of that government is to withdraw its ambassadors. According to protocol, it will not declare war and leave its ambassadors in enemy territory. I am personally convinced that God will not "declare war" until He has withdrawn His ambassadors from the earth. When He does, then I believe we will have never seen anything like what will come upon the earth.

I believe that when God's ambassadors are withdrawn, the message of reconciliation will no longer be offered. At that point there remains nothing but the final war between God and a Christ-rejecting earth led by the Antichrist and the harlot church. While we remain, however, we have the function, responsibilities and privileges of ambassadors. We are official representatives of heaven's government in an alien territory. When we speak, we proclaim the will of God with the authority that God has given us. In such cases, the whole authority of heaven is behind us, making our words good.

22

Restraining Corruption

As we have progressed in this book, we have discussed our responsibilities as Christians to be "the salt of the earth." The first characteristic of salt is to add flavor. What is the impact of that role? We flavor the world around us, making it palatable to the Lord.

The second attribute of salt to which the Church has been called is the restraining of corruption. Today, refrigeration is the most familiar means of preventing food from spoiling or corrupting. Before refrigeration, one main way of preserving foods, especially meat, was salt. For many centuries, sailors on long sea voyages had their meat preserved by salt. The presence of the salt restrained the forces of corruption to keep the meat edible for the duration of the voyage.

This is exactly what you and I are responsible to do. We are here to hold back the forces of corruption until God's purposes have been fulfilled. Corruption is already at work in the world. We cannot completely prevent it, but we may restrain it as long as "the voyage" lasts. When the purposes of God have been fulfilled, and we are withdrawn from the earth, then corruption will come to its head.

A Falling Away

Other than the book of Revelation, the second chapter of 2 Thessalonians probably contains the clearest statement about the coming of the one who is called *Antichrist*. Most of that chapter deals with the coming of this evil, satanically inspired and empowered ruler. Paul reminds Christians that the Antichrist cannot be manifested and the purpose of Satan cannot come to its culmination until something else first happens: "Let no one deceive you by any means; for that Day will not come unless the falling away comes first, and the man of sin is revealed, the son of perdition" (2 Thessalonians 2:3).

"The man of sin" and the "son of perdition" are two titles of the Antichrist. But please notice: The Antichrist cannot be revealed unless there is, first of all, a "falling away." This refers to a falling away from the Christian faith. The Greek word is *apostasia*, which gives us the English word *apostasy*. This word always signifies a turning away from the true faith of Jesus Christ. As long as believers retain the true faith, the man of sin cannot be revealed. Why? Because the believers are the salt holding back the final manifestation of corruption.

Believe me, Satan knows that this verse is in the Bible. He realizes that if he is going to manifest the Antichrist, he must first produce apostasy within the Church. In other words, the salt of the Church must lose its saltiness and thereby cease to fulfill its function. If the salt loses its saltiness, it ceases to resist corruption and the way is open for the manifestation of this final evil, satanic ruler.

We see, then, that one of Satan's main methods in fulfilling his objectives for the end of the age is to turn the believers away from the faith in apostasy. In the last half of the twentieth century there has been an apostasy within Christendom that could almost be called a landslide. In most major Protestant denominations, it has become acceptable to deny many of the basic tenets of the Christian faith. Actually, this apostasy can be traced directly to theological seminaries, many of which, in my opinion, are producing well-qualified apostates!

Years ago, I had the privilege of regular fellowship with Dennis Bennett, a pioneer in the charismatic renewal and the rector of St. Luke's Episcopal Mission Church in Seattle, Washington. I remember him recounting what he experienced when he went to a theological seminary in Chicago to be trained for the ministry. The very first professor he heard opened his lecture by declaring, "I want you to all understand clearly from the beginning that I'm an atheist." That was the first statement this teacher made to the students he was training in a seminary of Christian theology!

Seminaries have been a major instrument in breaking down the faith of many young men and women who initially had a desire to serve Christ. I have talked to many ministers who have been to seminary. Almost universally, they have stated that the hardest thing about seminary was to come out with any faith left! I have had others tell me, "It took me ten years to get out of me what seminary put in me before I could begin to serve Christ effectively." Tragically, many seminary graduates do not retain their faith.

I am not writing this to be malicious or uncharitable. I am merely stating what I believe to be simple, objective facts. Behind this "instruction in apostasy," we see the strategy of

Satan to turn away believers from faith—because until that happens, his purposes cannot be consummated. There must be a falling away whereby the salt loses its saltiness, allowing corruption to come to its head. This is exactly what is taking place in the world today. The apostates—the people who turn from the faith—are salt that has lost its savor.

Good for Nothing

Let's now see what happens to salt that has lost its savor. Jesus, continuing in the Sermon on the Mount, is speaking to the disciples who profess faith in Him: "You are the salt of the earth; but if the salt loses its flavor, how shall it be seasoned? It is then good for nothing but to be thrown out and trampled underfoot by men" (Matthew 5:13).

I do not believe you can find anything worse to say of a person than that he or she is "good for nothing." That, however, is precisely what Jesus says about believers who do not believe. They are good for nothing, and their destiny is to be cast out and to be trampled underfoot by men. Please notice that when Jesus says *men*, He refers to mankind. In due course the apostate church will be trampled underfoot. The Church in the United States and much of the Western culture today continues in the way of apostasy. If God does not intervene in revival, repentance and restoration, it will not be many years before Christians will indeed be trampled underfoot!

The only hope to avoid this outcome is the return of the Church to the true faith. The present move of the Holy Spirit taking place around the world is not simply a nice religious game. It is God's last offer of mercy, and people must understand this. There is nothing more grievous than to see so-called "Spirit-filled" believers treating their religious experience like a parlor game—like a spiritual alternative to a cocktail party.

I have had experiences in my own life that have shown me I must take my faith seriously because the forces of the enemy take their part very seriously. Satan is very much in earnest about wanting to destroy you and me. Believe me when I tell you that he is not playing games.

We do not have time for religious games. The people who are playing those games are playing them to their own destruction. Satan is out to destroy spirit, soul and body. He will attempt to torment you mentally and physically, breaking you and throwing you aside into the gutter like a squeezed orange when he is finished. When all we have to offer him is religious games he will laugh in our faces!

An Outbreak of Lawlessness

Let's return to 2 Thessalonians, where Scripture speaks about this man of sin being revealed: "And now you know what is restraining, that he may be revealed in his own time. For the mystery of lawlessness is already at work; only He who now restrains will do so until He is taken out of the way" (2 Thessalonians 2:6–7).

The Greek says literally, "Until he [the one who restrains] become out of the midst." That is an inelegant translation, but it is the literal meaning. In verse 6 Paul says, "*what* restrains," and in verse 7, he says, "*who* restrains." The restraining element is both a "what" and a "who."

I realize there are different opinions on this subject. But after many years of meditation, just letting the Lord speak to me, I believe that this refers to the presence of the Holy

Spirit as a Person within the Church of Jesus Christ. He is a "who" and He is a "what."

I do not say this for the sake of my own interest in the moving of the Spirit in our day, but because I believe it is of tremendous practical importance. *The* restraining influence that keeps back the final manifestation of Satan's purposes and the manifestation of the Antichrist as the world ruler is the third Person of the Trinity. It is the Holy Spirit in the Church.

In verse 7 Paul says, "The mystery of lawlessness is already at work." Corruption is already here, but the salt will hold the corruption back until the "voyage is finished." It is worth saying again: One major function of the salt of the true Church is to restrain corruption until God's purposes have been accomplished.

Lawlessness is something we see on a unique scale in all aspects of modern culture. Every day and night, the news carries a fresh record of meaningless lawlessness. Clearly, one reason for this outbreak of lawlessness is because there is apostasy within the Church. The salt is not doing its job.

In secular culture today, there almost seems to be a conspiracy to aid and abet the lawbreakers and hinder the law enforcers. We look at the Supreme Court of the United States and think, "Isn't that awful." But God says, "Look at the Church!" In actual fact, it is the *lawlessness of God's children within the Church*—the permissiveness of God's people within the Church—that opens the way for lawlessness and permissiveness in secular society. It is the failure of the salt that has produced the situation in the world. God does not blame the Supreme Court; He looks to the Church.

When the Church opens to lawlessness—when God's children behave like disobedient, disrespectful children—the children of the nation become disobedient, disrespectful children. What we dislike and criticize in much of modern youth is what God sees in His children in the Church. It is the spirit of lawlessness in the Church that spawns apostasy from the true faith and the standards of God, opening the way for lawlessness in the nation.

If My People

We all know the familiar verse—what God has said in 2 Chronicles 7:14: "If My people who are called by My name will humble themselves, and pray and seek My face, and turn from their wicked ways, then I will hear from heaven, and will forgive their sin and heal their land."

God is not speaking here to the unbeliever; He is speaking to His own people who are called by His name. He is speaking to Christians, upon whom the name of Christ is called. God's contention is with *His people*. If *His people* will meet His conditions, He will heal their land.

If God cannot reach His people, however, then the land cannot be healed. *We* are the salt of the earth, and the condition of our land reflects the condition of God's people. As long as we retain our saltiness, we hold back the corruption of lawlessness in society.

Luke 17:26 is a very simple verse. In that passage Jesus states, "As it was in the days of Noah, so it will be also in the days of the Son of Man." In previous chapters, we considered the condition of the world in the days of Noah and saw two prominent features: satanic, supernatural intervention in the spiritual realm and the breakdown of morals and ethics in the natural character of humankind. The earth was filled with violence, evil imaginations and sexual corruption.

We also saw that God had a restraining force at work—Noah and his family. Noah was a preacher of righteousness. But seven days before the flood actually began, God withdrew Noah and his family into the ark and closed the door. When the restraining force represented by Noah was withdrawn, iniquity, godlessness and lawlessness came to their climax. Then came judgment.

Jesus said it will be the same at the close of this age. God's representatives will be withdrawn, and for a short period of time lawlessness will be allowed to come to its climax. I believe, however, that this cannot happen until God's people have been withdrawn. Why? Because we are the salt of the earth.

The Holy Spirit as a Person came to earth on Pentecost to form a Body for Christ. When that Body is complete, the Holy Spirit will return to heaven, taking the Body of Christ with Him. Furthermore, I believe there is a unique situation in the world that started on the day of Pentecost. The third Person of the Godhead—the Holy Spirit—is actually personally resident here on earth, just as much as Jesus, the second Person of the Godhead, was here during the years of His earthly life. Jesus said, "I'll go away, but another Person will come. He'll take My place. He'll remain with you for the rest of the age" (see John 14:16).

Let me state something that I have personally come to believe. It would be altogether inconsistent with God's dignity that the final manifestation of Satan's power and authority would take place while the third Person of the Godhead is still personally resident here on earth. There will come a brief period when the Holy Spirit will have fulfilled His ministry, formed the Body of Christ, and He will take the Body with Him from the earth. When that happens, there will be a brief period (which we do not need to estimate in days or years) when lawlessness will come to its climax. At that time, God's judgment will be poured out without restraint as it was in the flood of Noah's day.

While we are here, we remain the salt of the earth. One of our supreme responsibilities, by everything we say and do, is to restrain the manifestation of the Antichrist and the consummation of lawlessness until God's purposes of grace have been fulfilled.

23

Casting Down Satan's Kingdom

In our discussion of the responsibilities we carry as the Church of Jesus Christ at the close of the age, we have talked about our key role in restraining Satan's activities and the corruption connected with it. In this chapter, our discussion will focus on the second responsibility that Jesus committed to His disciples: the power to cast down Satan's kingdom.

As a foundation for what we will share in this chapter, let's return to a familiar passage: "For we do not wrestle against flesh and blood, but against principalities, against powers, against the rulers of the darkness of this age, against spiritual hosts of wickedness in the heavenly places" (Ephesians 6:12).

As believers, we are involved in a wrestling match with satanic, spiritual rulers operating in the heavenlies. This is not the result of *our* failure or disobedience. It is part of God's program for us. We are committed to this wrestling match by the design and foreknowledge of almighty God. It is important for us to understand this, because there follows from it a logical consequence. If God by design has committed us to this wrestling match, then God has made victory possible for us. God would never deliberately commit His people to a conflict they could not win. If, therefore, it is the will of God for us to engage in this conflict, then the ultimate outcome can and should be total victory for the people of God.

Most Christians talk as if they are scared of the devil. But the truth is, if we remain in the right relationship to God without being boastful or presumptuous, it should be the devil who is afraid of us. In actuality, as a defeated foe he has only one tactic available to keep us from understanding our position of victory. The tactic he uses is *bluff*.

Removing Roadblocks

We are in a war. As we stated above, this is not because of failure on our part. It is part of the Church's calling and function. Let's look once again at 2 Corinthians 10:3–4: "For though we walk in the flesh, we do not war according to the flesh. For the weapons of our warfare are not carnal but mighty in God for pulling down strongholds."

When I was studying the word *strongholds*, I noticed that one meaning is "a kind of roadblock." Often when you move out into an aspect of God's purposes for you, you will meet resistance. (You remember, of course, that one of Satan's names is "the resister.") The resistance you encounter is a roadblock—and it is our commission to pull it down. In fact, as this verse attests, we have been given the weapons to do it.

The fact that Satan opposes something God leads you to do should be received as a compliment. *If what you were called to do by God were not important, Satan would not bother to oppose it.* Actually, I have found that one way to

158

discern the will of God is to notice what Satan opposes, because he always opposes the will of God.

Have you discovered this when you are moving out in the will of God into a new area of ministry or service? When you are undertaking new responsibilities, it can sometimes seem as if the whole world turns against you. If, like Job, the wind blows from every corner simultaneously, then you can be sure you are in the will of God!

God has given you the weapons to pull down every road-block that Satan raises in your path. Be sure, however, never to become afraid and turn round, exposing your back. God has provided every believer with weapons and armor to keep his or her front perfectly covered. But the back is totally exposed. The lesson? Never turn your back in fear! Keep facing the enemy and keep pressing on.

Boldness Required

Here is something that I believe strongly. If you are a child of God, you have the right to walk right down the center of the road and say, "Devil, stand aside. There's a child of God coming down the road. You have to move!" This is one hundred percent scriptural, because this is our right and our position in Jesus Christ. I believe we please God when we understand this boldness and use it. In general, I do not believe God is pleased by a lot of sniveling prayers: "O Lord, please . . ." There are genuine times to cry before the Lord, supplicating and laying hold upon God. But many times, God is most pleased when we accept our position in Christ, believe the authority Scripture gives us, and act accordingly with courage and boldness.

We see a wonderful example of such boldness in the book of Esther. There we read the story of the plot by Haman to exterminate the entire Jewish nation living in Persian exile. With judgment hanging over the Jewish people, Mordecai went out into the middle of the city and put on sackcloth. He himself had no access to King Ahasuerus. Esther, however, did. She put on her royal garments and went boldly right into the presence of the king. By her boldness, she changed the entire situation.

There are times when you can put on sackcloth for as long as you like. But one of the laws of the Kingdom is not to enter the King's gate clothed in sackcloth. If you will realize that you are a queen (a royal Bride), you can put on your beautiful garments and walk into the King's court with authority. The golden scepter will be held out to you and the King will say, "What can I do for you?"

God is delighted when we look to His Word. He is especially delighted when we believe boldly what His Word declares, even without evidence, circumstances, symptoms or any natural indications in the situation. God wants to say to us, "You're My partner. I want you to share My throne and tell Me what I can do for you." Any parent can realize how this pleases God. We do not want slavish, cowering obedience from our children. We want them to believe in our goodness, in our love for them, in our ability to provide for them and in our faithfulness. Should we believe that God wants any less of us?

Battles in Heavenly Places

Continuing our discussion of the battles we face, let's look at another picture from Scripture of this warfare in the heavenlies.

Daniel had given himself to a special three-week period of waiting upon God with mourning and fasting. "In those days I, Daniel, was mourning three full weeks. I ate no pleasant food, no meat or wine came into my mouth, nor did I anoint myself at all, till three whole weeks were fulfilled" (Daniel 10:2–3).

After seeking God for 21 days, God's answer came to him through a visitation by the angel Gabriel.

> Then he [Gabriel] said to me, "Do not fear, Daniel, for from the first day that you set your heart to understand, and to humble yourself before your God, your words were heard; and I have come because of your words. But the prince of the kingdom of Persia withstood me twenty-one days; and behold, Michael, one of the chief princes, came to help me, for I had been left alone there with the kings of Persia."
>
> Daniel 10:12–13

From the first day Daniel began to pray, his prayer had been heard and the angel had been sent with the answer. For three weeks, however, the messenger angel was held up in the heavenlies by the opposition of satanic angels. As fantastic as it may seem to the natural mind, it was Daniel's prayers that got the angel through. All Scripture bears testimony to this truth.

First of all, we must remember that the initiative was with earth, not with heaven. When Daniel started to pray on earth, heaven started to move. Second, the angel could not get through until Daniel prayed through. Daniel was involved in a major part of the conflict. A large part of it—not all of it, but much of it—rested upon Daniel and his prayers on earth rather than upon the warfare of angels in the heavenlies. I believe this is a preview of what it is going to be like for us and our active involvement in warfare at the close of this age.

The Final Outcome

In Revelation, we see the final fulfillment of the angelic warfare in the heavenlies. I am fully aware that various interpretations of this passage put it in the past, but I believe this has yet to be fulfilled.

> And war broke out in heaven: Michael and his angels fought with the dragon [the devil]; and the dragon and his angels fought [in the heavenlies], but they did not prevail, nor was a place found for them in heaven any longer. So the great dragon was cast out, that serpent of old, called the Devil and Satan, who deceives the whole world; he was cast to the earth, and his angels were cast out with him.
>
> Revelation 12:7–9

This is the point that marks the first time Satan loses his place in the heavenlies. Up until this time the headquarters of Satan and his hosts remain in the heavenly places. Because this time has not yet come, they are still positioned in heavenly places, accusing and resisting the purposes of God.

> Then I heard a loud voice saying in heaven, "Now salvation, and strength, and the kingdom of our God, and the power [Greek, authority] of His Christ have come, for the accuser of our brethren, who accused them before our God day and night, has been cast down [from the heavenlies]. And they overcame him by the blood of the Lamb and by the word of their testimony, and they did not love their lives to the death."
>
> Revelation 12:10–11

The authority of Christ will have been made totally effective in the heavenlies when Satan is cast down. This is still in the future. For now, Satan is still accusing you and me who are believers in Christ. But notice that the final culmination of Satan's being cast down is attributed to the believers on earth. The believers on earth overcame Satan by weapons that angels could not use: the blood of the Lamb and the word of their testimony.

Angels really do not have testimonies, but sinners do. *We* overcome Satan by the blood of the Lamb and the word of our testimony. In other words, the final casting down of Satan and his angels from their place in the heavenlies is the responsibility of the believers on earth! How we apply this will be the subject of the next few chapters of this study.

There is one final phase of this spiritual conflict, and that is the destruction of Satan's forces on earth. This act of destruction is left to Jesus when He appears in His glory. There will be a short period after Satan is cast down from heaven when he will have his headquarters on earth. That is when he will make the greatest amount of trouble for anybody he possibly can. Why? Because he knows in those days that he has very little time left.

After that period of trouble, however, Jesus will come from heaven and deal personally with Satan and the Antichrist: "And then the lawless one will be revealed, whom the Lord will consume with the breath of His mouth and destroy with the brightness of His coming" (2 Thessalonians 2:8).

Jesus' final victory over Satan is not the topic of this study. The important thing for us to see in this teaching is that restraining Satan's work and the casting down of Satan and his angels from heaven is our responsibility in this age.

Since we are engaged in this spiritual warfare—whether we like it or not—we need to be familiar with the weapons God has placed at our disposal. What resources have we been given—especially in our personal lives—to overcome evil? How will we be part of the final casting down of Satan as pictured in Revelation 12? In the next chapter we will begin to answer those questions.

24

The Blood, the Word and Our Testimony

In our study thus far we have seen that the Lord Jesus Christ
has committed two special end time responsibilities to His
disciples on earth. First of all, we have been called to restrain
the outworking of Satan's purposes on earth until God's purposes of grace have been fulfilled. Second, we have been commissioned to cast down Satan's kingdom from the heavenlies.

On the basis of His work on the cross, Jesus has given us
authority to trample on all the representatives of Satan's kingdom and to overcome all the power of the enemy. In connection with that assignment, Jesus added the beautiful promise,
"Nothing will harm you" (see Luke 10:19). In other words,
"You don't need to be afraid. Believe in me and do what I command, and you will see My victory worked out in your lives."

Our Spiritual Weapons

Knowing that the victory has already been won through
Jesus, we need to examine the spiritual weapons that God has
provided for our spiritual warfare—weapons that guarantee

total victory if used in faith. Since our warfare is spiritual, our weapons must correspond as spiritual weapons.

> For though we walk in the flesh, we do not war according to the flesh. For the weapons of our warfare are not carnal but mighty in God for pulling down strongholds, casting down arguments and every high thing that exalts itself against the knowledge of God, bringing every thought into captivity to the obedience of Christ.
>
> 2 Corinthians 10:3–5

Our weapons, Paul writes, are not of the flesh. This implies they are spiritual. Furthermore, they are divinely powerful, meaning they have the power of God Himself in them, enabling us to destroy Satan's strongholds. Please note: The Bible does not picture us as being on the defensive. Rather, we are to be on the attack. We are not cowering behind our church walls, wondering what Satan can do against us. Rather we are out on the offensive, destroying Satan's fortresses. Wherever Satan raises a fortress—something lofty, proud, arrogant, asserting his kingdom and his claims—that is the place where we fight. We are able to move against these efforts of the enemy with the weapons God has given us—and by them, we destroy his fortresses.

Because our warfare is not in the carnal or material realm, our weapons are not carnal or material. They are not guns, tanks or fighter jets; they are spiritual weapons for spiritual warfare. In verse 5, Paul says that through these weapons we can cast down every high thing that has exalted itself against the knowledge of God. This is an amazing statement that we can read many times without appreciating its full ramifications. The one "high thing" above all others that is exalted against the knowledge of God is Satan's kingdom in the heavenlies.

At the close of the previous chapter, we saw from Revelation 12 that there will be a great conflict enacted in the heavenlies at the close of this age. From Revelation 12:7 and onward, we read that there will be war in heaven. Michael and his angels will be opposing the devil and his angels. As a result of this final conflict in the heavenlies, the devil and his angels will be cast down to the earth. Amazingly, the final culminating power that brings the satanic angels down from the heavenlies is the power of the spiritual weapons used by believers on earth.

God has provided many marvelous weapons, but I want to focus on what I believe to be the most powerful weapons of all. I say this not only on the basis of Scripture but also on the basis of my own personal experience. I am not offering just theology or theory. I am sharing out of experiences and facts that I have proved in my own life and ministry.

The Blood and the Word

Revelation 12:11 presents the spiritual weapons we must utilize: "And they [believers on earth] overcame him [Satan] by the blood of the Lamb and by the word of their testimony, and they did not love their lives to the death." The Lamb identified here is "the Lamb of God who takes away the sin of the world" (John 1:29). The Lamb of God is the Lord Jesus Christ. The blood, therefore, is the blood of Jesus. Then there is the personal testimony of the believers, which is centered in the Word—the Word of God.

I hear many people talk about "pleading the blood" or declaring "it's under the blood" and so on. In many cases, however, these are nothing but religious phrases because there is no practical application. Other people even talk about overcoming Satan by the blood of the Lamb and the word of their testimony. It sounds good. It certainly is scriptural. But what does it really mean? Over the years I have meditated on this topic, and I have come up with the following statement that I believe to be the correct explanation. *We must testify personally to what the Word says that the blood does for us.*

Testifying is the personal action that makes this truth operative. *If we do not testify, nothing goes into operation.* Our personal testimony is the action that triggers the whole process and brings Satan's defeat. I believe this is why we often experience a special kind of opposition when we begin to testify—because at that point we are beginning to do the devil some harm. As far as the devil is concerned, you may believe whatever you like. He is not greatly disturbed by it until you begin to testify the Word of God. When you start to testify, the enemy is going to do everything he can to discourage and frighten you. He wants to keep you from declaring the Word of God, because it is your testifying that makes these weapons effective.

Exactly what is denoted by *the blood of the Lamb* is illustrated from one of the great patterns in the Old Testament. The first thought a Jewish person will have upon hearing or reading the words *the blood of the lamb* is the yearly Passover ceremony that commemorates Israel's deliverance out of bondage in Egypt. I believe the greatest single type or pattern of the blood of Christ and its power is the sacrifice of the Passover lamb for Israel when they were in Egypt.

The Passover Lamb

Israel's deliverance from bondage was based on the blood of the lamb being applied to their homes. Exodus 12:6–7 speaks about a lamb that every Israelite father chose for his household:

> "Now you shall keep it until the fourteenth day of the same month. Then the whole assembly of the congregation of Israel shall kill it at twilight. And they shall take some of the blood and put it on the two doorposts and on the lintel of the houses where they eat it."

The Lord told the children of Israel why this was necessary:

> "For I will pass through the land of Egypt on that night, and will strike all the firstborn in the land of Egypt, both man and beast; and against all the gods of Egypt I will execute judgment: I am the LORD. Now the blood shall be a sign for you on the houses where you are. And when I see the blood, I will pass over you; and the plague shall not be on you to destroy you when I strike the land of Egypt."
>
> Exodus 12:12–13

Moses explained the exact details of how the blood was to be applied. It is obvious that if you simply kill a lamb out in the open, its blood will pour out onto the ground. This Scripture makes it clear that when the lamb was killed, its blood was to be caught carefully in a basin where it could be available for use.

> Then Moses called for all the elders of Israel and said to them, "Pick out and take lambs for yourselves according to your families, and kill the Passover lamb. And you shall take a bunch of hyssop, dip it in the blood that is in the basin, and strike the lintel and the two doorposts with the blood that is in the basin. And none of you shall go out of the door of his house until morning. For the LORD will pass through to strike the Egyptians; and when He sees the blood on the

lintel and on the two doorposts, the LORD will pass over the door and not allow the destroyer to come into your houses to strike you."

Exodus 12:21–23

The word *pass over* in Hebrew is the same word for the Passover celebration. It is called Passover because the Lord passed over the houses on which the blood was applied. Notice that the people were not saved because they were Israelites. Being of natural descent from Abraham did not protect them. The only protection for Israel was meeting the requirements concerning their use of the blood of the lamb.

Each Israelite father took the lamb for his household and killed it. Its blood was caught in a basin. At that point, the sacrifice was complete and the blood was available. But having blood in the basin did not protect a single Israelite family. They could have all killed a lamb, caught the blood and left it in the basin—and the same judgment that came upon the Egyptians would have come upon them.

A Vital Transfer

God required that the blood be transferred from the basin to the most conspicuous place in the front of every Israelite home: the door. God commanded that the blood be applied to the lintel and to both side posts of the doorframe. It was not to be applied to the threshold, however, because the blood was never to be placed where it could be trodden upon. This would have been a sign of great irreverence (see Hebrews 10:29).

The blood was to be applied where it could be plainly visible to anyone who passed by. God said, "When I see the blood upon the lintel and on the doorposts, then I will pass over you and I will not suffer the destroyer to enter into you."

Here is the critical application for each of us: Only when the blood was transferred from the basin to the door did it protect the Israelite family that lived inside that house. How does this picture from the Old Testament Passover apply to our spiritual warfare against Satan? In particular, how do we exercise the authority given us to avail ourselves of the blood?

Before we consider these questions, let's clarify a point. In the New Testament, the Passover lamb was a picture of Jesus, the Lamb of God. All that was revealed in the type, or picture, about the Passover lamb was fulfilled in Jesus, the Lamb of God, through His death on the cross. Two Scriptures make this clear. First, in John 1:29, John the Baptist is preparing the way for Jesus: "The next day John saw Jesus coming toward him, and said, 'Behold! The Lamb of God who takes away the sin of the world!'"

By revelation John the Baptist pointed out to the people of his time that Jesus was the Lamb of God who would take away the sin of the world. Every Israelite who heard that phrase *the Lamb of God* was immediately reminded, because of his background and his tradition, of that unique, sacred ceremony of the Passover lamb.

Second, in 1 Corinthians 5:7, Paul writes, "For indeed Christ, our Passover, was sacrificed for us." This is a fact of history. When Jesus died on the cross He was the Lamb of God taking away the sin of the world. He was the Passover Lamb who was slain and who by His blood made available total protection and total victory to all the people of God.

The application that is of vital personal importance for every one of us is that *Jesus has already been sacrificed and*

His blood has already been shed. Applying the "type" of the Old Testament Passover, the blood is in the basin. It is available. Just as the blood in the basin had to be applied personally to each home, the same is true for us. The fact that Christ has died and shed His blood on the cross must be applied personally—by faith—by every believer.

Applying the Blood

By the command of God, the Israelites were given only one means to transfer the blood from the basins to the doors of their homes. They were told to use a little bunch of hyssop, a plant that grows everywhere in the Middle East. They had to pluck the hyssop, dip the hyssop in the blood in the basin and then strike the hyssop against the lintel and the doorposts. In so doing the blood came off the hyssop and remained on the door.

A similar principle applies to us as New Testament believers. We believe in Jesus Christ as the Lamb of God. We believe His blood has been shed and everything we need is available through His blood. As long as the blood of Christ remains "in the basin," however, it does not bring us its full benefit. The benefits are there potentially, but an effective application is required.

In the Old Covenant, God gave Israel one means to transfer the blood: a bunch of hyssop. In the New Covenant we, of course, do not use hyssop. What then corresponds to the hyssop for us as New Testament believers? What makes the blood available and effective in our lives? The answer is in Revelation 12:11: *It is the word of our testimony*. When I testify about the blood of Jesus, I make the blood available to my situation.

My testimony about the blood in a New Covenant setting is exactly analogous to the Israeli father in the Old Covenant setting as he dipped the hyssop in the basin and struck it on the doorposts of his home. There is complete, total and perfect protection in the blood of the Lamb, the Lord Jesus Christ. We must learn to testify personally to what the Word of God says the blood of Jesus does. Otherwise, we will not have the full benefits from the blood.

Testimony Is Our Hyssop

From the points I have just shared with you, God has revealed to me one of the most precious, practical and effective truths for my own life. *In order to transfer the blood of Jesus to the place where we need protection and victory, we do not use hyssop. We use our personal testimony.* Our testimony in the New Testament takes the place of the hyssop in the Old Testament. We transfer the blood of Jesus to our lives when we testify personally to what the Word of God says the blood of Jesus does for us.

These three different weapons, when put together, bring total victory: the blood of the Lamb, the Word of God and our personal testimony—what we ourselves say with our own mouths. The blood of the Lamb, since the time when Jesus was slain, is always available in the basin. The Word of God never changes; it is unvarying. The variable factor in this operation is our testimony.

Our testimony corresponds to the hyssop. It is something simple. It is something available to everybody. And yet, it is crucial. Without the hyssop, the blood of the Passover lamb did nothing for anybody. It was available but it was ineffective. Likewise, in the New Covenant, the blood of Christ is available. Everything we will ever need is provided through the blood, and all its provisions are revealed through the Word. It is our testimony, however, that makes it effective.

I am sure you can now see why the battle centers around your testimony. The moment you begin to testify, Satan will throw at you everything at his disposal—to frighten you, to make you feel shy, embarrassed or ashamed. He will use any method possible to prevent you from coming out with a clear, bold, scriptural testimony. Why? Because when you testify effectively, he cannot touch you anymore. Just as the destroyer in the Old Testament times was not allowed to pass in, under or through the blood of the Passover lamb, your testimony keeps Satan from touching you.

Clearly, in order to defeat Satan in the end times by testifying personally to what the Word says the blood does, it is essential that we know what the Word says about the blood. That will be our focus for the remainder of this book.

25

What the Blood Does

In our previous chapter, we focused on the power of our testimony. We discovered the statement that is the key to our victory as outlined in Revelation 12:11. Here it is: *We overcome the enemy when we testify personally to what the Word says that the blood does for us.* How can we testify to a truth unless we know it for ourselves? In the closing short chapters of this book, we will consider specific statements of Scripture concerning what the blood of Jesus does for us as believers. Not only will we briefly examine these truths, but we will also put them into practice by declaring them as our own personal testimony.

Redemption

The first Scripture we will consider is Ephesians 1:7: "In Him [Jesus] we have redemption through His blood, the forgiveness of sins, according to the riches of His grace."

In order to receive these benefits, we must be "in Christ"—true believers. When we are in Christ, the first benefit we have is redemption through His blood. To redeem means "to buy back, to pay a ransom price." When we were in the hands of the devil, we belonged to him. But Jesus paid the ransom price of His blood on the cross to buy us back. This is confirmed in 1 Peter 1:18–19:

> Knowing that you were not redeemed with corruptible things, like silver or gold, from your aimless conduct received by tradition from your fathers, but with the precious blood of Christ, as of a lamb without blemish and without spot.

When we were redeemed, we were bought back from our old, evil, ungodly way of living. We were rescued from the grip of Satan, from the condemnation of sin and from being open to the attacks of the devourer and the destroyer. We were redeemed by the precious blood of Jesus Christ as a Lamb who took away the sin of the world. It is only through His blood that we are redeemed; there was no other price that could redeem us. In light of that great redemption, Psalm 107:2 declares: "Let the redeemed of the LORD say so, whom He has redeemed from the hand of the enemy."

Personally, I know full well that I was in the devil's hand before Jesus touched my life. I have no doubt whatsoever about that. I know what it is like to be in the devil's hand, and I never want to be there again. I also know that it was the blood of Jesus that redeemed me out of the hand of the devil and into the hand of the Good Shepherd. And I know something else: Jesus said, "Neither shall anyone snatch them out of My hand" (John 10:28).

Psalm 91 has been called "the atomic psalm" because this psalm is powerful! It promises perfect protection from every kind of evil, danger and harm. We are protected from enemy attack—however it may come, by whatever means and at whatever time. We see this truth from reading the first two verses: "He who dwells in the secret place of the Most High shall abide under the shadow of the Almighty. I will say of the Lord, 'He is my refuge and my fortress; my God, in Him I will trust.'"

The word *abide* in Hebrew normally means "to pass the night" and is frequently used in that way. During the hours of darkness, therefore, the true believer will be under the shadow or protection of the Almighty.

When the psalmist says, "I will say," this is the entrance—the way—into the complete protection of the remaining verses. Your testimony begins: "I will say." You need to say it to possess it. It takes some courage to step into the protection that follows in Psalm 91. Yet only those who say it have the scriptural right to live in it. It is the word of our testimony that makes it effective.

Here, then, is our testimony in the light of Ephesians 1:7 and Psalm 107:2.

> *Through the blood of Jesus, I am redeemed*
> *out of the hand of the devil.*

Please stop reading at this point and declare this proclamation with boldness. When you do, you are "applying the blood on your doorposts."

Forgiveness

Returning to Ephesians 1:7, we notice a second statement about the blood: "In Him we have redemption through His blood, *the forgiveness of sins*, according to the riches of His grace" (emphasis added).

Not only are we redeemed by the blood, but we also have the forgiveness of our sins. Let's remind ourselves of what Jesus said at the Last Supper as He gave His disciples the cup, which was the emblem of His blood: "For this is My blood of the new covenant, which is shed for many for the remission [forgiveness] of sins" (Matthew 26:28).

Hebrews 9:22 tells us, "Without shedding of blood there is no remission [of sin]." This is a pattern repeated throughout Scripture. The blood of Jesus was shed that our sins might be forgiven.

In Ephesians 1:7, Paul makes these two truths coextensive: redemption through His blood and the forgiveness of sins. This is an important point to understand, because we have the full legal rights of redemption only insofar as our sins are forgiven. If all our sins are forgiven, we have the total rights of redemption. If, however, there is unconfessed and unforgiven sin in our lives, we do not have the full legal rights of redemption in that area. In effect, Satan still has a legal claim over that part of our lives.

I have seen the truth of this principle many times in the ministry of deliverance. If Satan has a legal claim, he will not give it up. You can shout in his face, fast for a week and pray all you like. None of that will move him because he knows he has a legal claim that still has not been settled in that area through forgiveness.

Another common reason why believers give Satan a legal claim in their lives is their failure to forgive others. Jesus taught us that we are forgiven by God to the same degree we forgive others: "Forgive us our debts, as we forgive our debtors" (Matthew 6:12).

We are not entitled to claim forgiveness from God beyond the measure to which we forgive others. If, therefore, there is any person we have not forgiven, neither are we forgiven by God. Essentially, when we refuse to forgive others, we allow Satan to have yet another legal claim. Do what you will, you cannot dislodge him until you have forgiven the one you need to forgive. Remember this about the devil: He is a legal expert and he knows it. God's Word, however, offers us total forgiveness of sin, and it is most important that we hold on to the total forgiveness by faith.

In the light of Ephesians 1:7, if I am willing to confess and renounce all sin, the process works. If I am willing to forgive all other persons who have hurt or wronged me, as I would have God forgive me, on that basis I am then able to make this second testimony:

Through the blood of Jesus, all my sins are forgiven.

That testimony, when we make it personally with our own lips, is like the hyssop. It transfers the blood from the basin to the place where we need it in our own hearts and lives. I encourage you to stop reading at this point, and declare this statement out loud. Say it boldly and with conviction!

If you made that confession, then you have applied the work of the blood of Jesus to your life in a practical and biblical way. Even if you cannot sense it or feel it, something took place in the spiritual realm. The forces of Satan were compelled to take a step in retreat before the power of the blood of Jesus.

26

Cleansing

We will now look at our third scriptural statement. The Word of God says this about what the blood of the Lamb accomplishes in us: "If we walk in the light as He is in the light, we have fellowship with one another, and the blood of Jesus Christ His Son cleanses us from all sin" (1 John 1:7).

Before we consider the application of the blood in this passage, please notice three interrelated practices that cannot be separated. What are they? Walking in the light, fellowship one with another and the cleansing of the blood. Over the years, I have met scores of people who claim the cleansing and protection of the blood, but who did not meet the conditions that entitle them to receive it.

The cleansing of the blood of Jesus Christ is a consequence that follows an act introduced by the word *if*. In other words, the experience of the promise is conditional upon the fulfillment of the stated condition. *If* we walk in the light as He is in the light, then two results follow: We have fellowship one with another, and the blood of Jesus cleanses us from all sin.

Logically, if we are not in fellowship with one another, it is proof we are not walking in the light. It follows that if we are not walking in the light, we cannot claim the cleansing of the blood of Jesus. We come, therefore, to this conclusion: If we are out of fellowship with one another, we are out of the light. Additionally, if we are out of the light, the blood no longer cleanses us. *The blood of Jesus cleanses only in the light.* This is one of the most important principles in the Word of God. We must come to grips with it!

I have heard scores of Christians deceive themselves about their right of access to the blood, quoting 1 John 1:7. Yet they never fulfilled the condition stated in the *if*. We must walk in the light as He is in the light. The evidence that we are walking in the light is that we have fellowship one with another. Fellowship is the place of light, which is why fellowship is the place of testing. The closer we walk in fellowship, the brighter the light grows—until there are no hidden corners, no shadows, nothing swept under the rug and nothing covered up.

That is a frightening place. But it is the only place where the blood of Jesus fully fulfills its function of cleansing. If you desire full cleansing from sin, it is in the light. If, however, you are in any way wrongly aligned with God or with your neighbor, then you are not fully in the light.

Coming into the light means confessing our sins and bringing them into the light. This is one of the hardest steps for us to take. We naturally shrink from this practice. But here is the truth: When sin gets into the light, it disappears—because the blood cleanses it. If we do not bring it to the light, then we keep it. This is a tremendously important principle. The blood operates only in the light.

If we have met the conditions, then you and I have the right to make this testimony:

*As I walk in the light, the blood of Jesus
is cleansing me now—and continually—from all sin.*

Never leave out that little word *all*. It is important, especially when we are talking about sin. There are no sins beyond the reach of the blood of Jesus. Each and every sin is included. When we make our testimony personally with our own lips, it is like the hyssop. It transfers the blood from the basin to the place where we need it—to our own hearts and lives.

I encourage you to stop reading at this point and declare this statement out loud. Speak it out boldly and with conviction: *As I walk in the light, the blood of Jesus is cleansing me now—and continually—from all sin.* Having made that confession, you have applied the work of the blood of Jesus to your life in a personal, practical way.

As you make that confession, meeting the conditions, the spiritual atmosphere changes. You are protected and cleansed from the pollution of the spiritual environment around you.

Why have I asked you to make these confessions at each stage of our study? Because I want these wonderful truths to be more than just knowledge—more than just something you have learned. To be effective in your life, they must be used and practiced every day.

27

Justification

As we have seen in the previous chapters, we overcome Satan when we testify personally to what the Word of God says the blood of Jesus does for us. A fourth, and very important, provision of the blood of Jesus is our *justification*. In Romans 5:8–9, Paul writes to the believers in Rome: "But God demonstrates His own love toward us, in that while we were still sinners, Christ died for us. Much more then, having now been justified by His blood, we shall be saved from wrath through Him."

We are *justified* by the blood of Jesus. Justified is one of those religious words that many people use without knowing its full meaning. Often, we do not really understand the term, and may even find it a little scary. Wherever you read the word *justified* in the Bible, you can substitute the word *righteous*. This is true in the Old Testament Hebrew as well as in the New Testament Greek. Bible translators alternately translate the same word *righteous* or *justified* depending on the context. When it is a matter of legal processes, they tend to use the word *just*. When it is a matter of practical living, they tend to use the word *righteous*. Whichever translation is used, it is the same word.

What It Means

The problem with the use of the word *justified* is that people tend to reserve it for a legal transaction. It is as if somewhere up in the dusty courts of heaven, some mysterious transaction happened and now everything is all right. This is only taking into account half the meaning of the word.

To be justified means "to be made righteous." I prefer the word *righteous* because it brings it right down to where I live: my home, my business and my personal relationships. *Justified* sounds like a legal formality that has to be transacted in some remote court somewhere—one that does not have much application to my living. But *righteous* brings it immediately to daily life.

Scripture says—and this is a perfectly legitimate and correct translation—that we have been made righteous by the blood of Jesus. In truth, you are not justified if you have not been made righteous. It is more than a legal ceremony. It is more than a change of labels. It is a transformation of character and life produced by the blood of Jesus. Remember the definition we used earlier? If I am justified, it is *"just-as-if-I'd"* never sinned. How can we say that? Because we have been made righteous with a righteousness that is not our own—the righteousness of Jesus Christ.

Romans 3:24–25 adds to our understanding: "Being justified [made righteous] freely by His grace through the redemption that is in Christ Jesus, whom God set forth as a propitiation by His blood, through faith. . . ." I am glad the word *freely* is in this verse. The problem with religious people is that they are always trying to earn the favor of God. Ironically, they never feel they do enough to obtain it. They are never satisfied, nor are they ever really relaxed—because they think they must do just a little bit more to be made righteous. This will never work because we are justified only through faith in the blood of Jesus.

Romans 4:4–5 continues this: "Now to him who works, the wages are not counted as grace but as debt. But to him who does not work but believes on Him who justifies the ungodly, his faith is accounted for righteousness."

If we believe that we have always lived right and always done our duty, we might feel that God owes righteousness to us as a debt. In fact, God does not owe anything to anybody. That is why Paul says "to him who does not work."

The first step you must take to obtain righteousness is to *stop doing anything*. Stop trying to make yourself righteous. Stop trying to be a little better. Call a halt to it all. "To him who does not work." What must you do? Just believe! Can it be that simple? If it is not that simple, we will never make it! God makes unrighteous people righteous. That is what Scripture says, and we must believe it.

The Exchange

The fact that we have been given the righteousness of God is clearly stated by Paul: "For He made Him [Jesus] who knew no sin to be sin for us, that we might become the righteousness of God in Him" (2 Corinthians 5:21). There is the complete exchange. Jesus was made sin with our sinfulness that we might be made righteous with His righteousness. His righteousness is available through faith in His blood.

Righteousness produces certain immediate and definite observable results in our lives. Actually, the whole of our living—our attitude, our relationships, and the effectiveness of our Christian life and service—will depend on how far we realize that we have been made righteous.

Proverbs 28:1 declares, "The wicked flee when no one pursues, but the righteous are bold as a lion." Many Christians today are not as bold as they might be. They are timid, apologetic, and tend to back down when confronted with evil or the devil. The root cause for many is that they have not appreciated the fact that they are righteous in God's sight, as righteous as Jesus Christ Himself. When we appreciate and apprehend that truth, it makes us bold.

Isaiah 32:17 tells us: "The work of righteousness will be peace, and the effect of righteousness, quietness and assurance forever."

Here are three products of righteousness: peace, quietness and assurance. They all come from the realization that I have been made righteous with the righteousness of Jesus Christ. Righteousness brings boldness, peace, quietness and assurance.

Romans 14:17 is a familiar Scripture to most of us: "For the kingdom of God is not eating and drinking, but righteousness and peace and joy in the Holy Spirit."

All these benefits are products of righteousness. If we do not receive the righteousness of Christ by faith, then we will struggle for all these other benefits and never achieve them. It is pathetic to see Christians trying to be joyful, trying to have peace, trying to relax and trying to be assured because somebody has told them that is how they ought to be.

I have observed that when a believer truly lays hold of the assurance of the forgiveness of sin and righteousness by faith, these results just happen. Joy flows naturally, peace is not an effort, assurance is there and boldness expresses itself. The root problem is getting people to realize they have been made righteous with the righteousness of Jesus Christ, justified, "just-as-if-I'd" never sinned.

A Positive Declaration

It is ironic that many religious people actually think they are more holy if they focus on how sinful they are! It reflects a prevalent religious attitude that anyone making a claim to be righteous is conceited. In that view, you are very religious if you keep speaking about your failures, your inconsistencies and how many things you do wrong.

I was brought up in a church where we were taught to do just that. Every Sunday morning we had to say, "Pardon us, miserable offenders." But I never felt that I wanted to be a "miserable offender." When I looked at the other offenders, I surely agreed they were miserable! But I eventually said to myself, *If all religion can do is make me a miserable offender, I can be an offender without religion and not half so miserable!* When I made that realization, that is what I eventually became—an offender without religion.

That statement I so despised is so much the language of religion: "Pardon us, miserable offenders. We have erred and strayed from Thy ways like lost sheep; we have done those sins which we ought not to have done; and we have left undone those things which we ought to have done. And there is no health in us."

I could not say those words now, because I would be a hypocrite to say them. First of all, I believe I have divine health in Jesus Christ. Second, how could I pray for victory over sin on Monday morning if I know that six days later, on Sunday morning, I would be making the same statement? How could I be victorious and keep saying that I erred and strayed? Having done those things that I ought not have done and left undone those things I ought to have done? This type of language completely undermines the basis of my faith, and yet it sounds so good. You may be horrified when you read this, but I mean every word of it. I lived through twenty years of that kind of religion and it was enough!

Let's come to our testimony according to what the Bible says rather than what some human institution teaches. Here is our testimony according to the Word of God:

> ***Through the blood of Jesus, I am justified, made righteous, "just-as-if-I'd" never sinned.***

There is no room for guilt or shame in that statement. Again, please stop reading at this point and declare this testimony in faith for yourself. Continue to confess this until you know you are free from all guilt concerning your sin. The kind of righteousness I have received through faith in the blood of Jesus does not admit guilt. I can stand before God without shame, without spot, and I can answer Satan with total boldness: "Satan, it's in vain for you to accuse me because I am not meeting you in my own righteousness; I am meeting you in the righteousness I've received by faith in the blood of Jesus, the righteousness of God that is without spot, without sin and without stain." That is our testimony!

Thus far we have four testimonies by which we may overcome the activity of evil in our lives:

Through the blood of Jesus, I am redeemed out of the hand of the devil.

Through the blood of Jesus, all my sins are forgiven.

As I walk in the light, the blood of Jesus is cleansing me now—and continually—from all sin.

Through the blood of Jesus, I am justified, made righteous, "just-as-if-I'd" never sinned.

I trust you are beginning to understand that you can add anything you like to your testimony that is in Scripture. You can say, for instance, "Through the blood of Jesus, I overcome the devil." Stop your reading for just a moment and say that in victory and triumph, "Through the blood of Jesus, I overcome the devil." Now, praise God and thank Him for what the blood of Jesus has done for you. The more you thank Him, the more real it becomes.

28

Sanctification

The fifth benefit of the blood of Jesus is *sanctification*. We will look at two verses in Hebrews that speak about the sanctifying power of the blood of Jesus. First is Hebrews 10:29, which speaks about the apostate, a person who turns back from the Christian faith after having known it, into deliberate denial and rejection of the Lord Jesus Christ. The writer speaks about all the sacred things that the apostate renounces and, in a sense, defiles.

> Of how much worse punishment, do you suppose, will he be thought worthy who has trampled the Son of God underfoot, counted the blood of the covenant by which he was sanctified a common thing, and insulted the Spirit of grace?

Please notice that this verse speaks, in a sense, about treading underfoot the blood of Jesus. You will remember our reference to the Passover event when the blood was applied to the lintel and the doorposts, but not to the threshold where it could be stepped upon. We are never to show disrespect for the blood of Jesus. Here, however, is a person who has been sanctified by the blood of the New Covenant and then turns back. The point of this passage, for our purposes, is not the people who turn back, but the fact that we are sanctified by the blood of the covenant.

In Hebrews 13:12, the same truth is brought out: "Therefore Jesus also, that He might sanctify the people with His own blood, suffered outside the gate." Again we see that the blood of Jesus sanctifies the believer. *Sanctifies* is another religious word that can cause misunderstanding. The word *sanct* is a Latin root word related directly to the word *saint*. It is another way of translating the Greek word *holy*. *To sanctify*, therefore, means "to make saintly" or "to make holy." To be sanctified is to be made holy. The idea of holiness always includes within it the meaning of being set apart to God. Sanctification, like righteousness, does not come by good works, greater efforts or more religion. It comes by faith in the blood of Jesus: "Jesus, that He might *sanctify the people with His blood*, suffered outside the gate."

Kept Away by the Blood

The one who is sanctified is in a place where God has access to him, but the devil does not. To be sanctified is to be removed from the area of Satan's visitation and reach. You are placed in an area where you are available to God; however, you are not at home when the devil calls. To be sanctified is to belong to God, to be under God's control and to be available to Him. Anything that is not of God has no right of approach to you. It is kept away by the blood.

In this connection, Paul writes:

> Giving thanks to the Father who has qualified us to be partakers of the inheritance of the saints in the light. He has delivered us

from the power [Greek, authority] of darkness and conveyed [translated, KJV] us into the kingdom of the Son of His love.

Colossians 1:12–13

Notice, first of all, that darkness has power or authority. Satan has authority over the disobedient because of their disobedience. Through faith in the blood of Jesus, however, we have been removed from the area of Satan's authority, and translated into the Kingdom of God and of Jesus Christ. The NKJV uses the word *conveyed*, but I prefer the King James word *translated* because it gives a more vivid description.

The word *translate* means "to carry over from one place to another place." In Scripture it is used to speak of a total transfer from one place to another. I mentioned earlier that in the Old Testament two men were translated from earth to heaven: Enoch and Elijah. Both of them were translated entirely. All that Elijah left behind was his mantle; his body went with him.

As I understand Scripture, this is the truth for what God has done for us in Christ. We are not *going* to be, we *have been* totally translated: spirit, soul and body. We are no longer in the devil's territory. We are not under the devil's laws. We are in the territory of the Son of God and under His laws.

The devil's law is stated in Romans 8:2: "the law of sin and death." The law of God's Kingdom is stated in the same verse: "the law of the Spirit of life in Christ Jesus." This verse says, "The law of the Spirit of life in Christ Jesus has made me free from the law of sin and death."

Because we are set apart to God, we are not in the devil's territory or under his law of sin and death. His kingdom no longer applies to us, because we are in another Kingdom. We have been translated, carried over, spirit, soul and body. We are sanctified, set apart to God through the blood of Jesus.

Set Apart

I want to show again, from the pattern of the Passover, how the blood of the Passover lamb sanctified Israel by setting them apart to God in a specific way.

> Then Moses said, "Thus says the LORD: 'About midnight I will go out into the midst of Egypt; and all the firstborn in the land of Egypt shall die, from the firstborn of Pharaoh who sits on his throne, even to the firstborn of the female servant who is behind the handmill, and all the firstborn of the animals. Then there shall be a great cry throughout all the land of Egypt, such as was not like it before, nor shall be like it again. But against none of the children of Israel shall a dog move its tongue, against man or beast, that you may know that the LORD does make a difference between the Egyptians and Israel.'"
>
> Exodus 11:4–7

Notice that the Lord made a distinction between His people and those who were not His people. Wrath and judgment came upon those who were not God's people. But God's people were so protected that not even a dog would bark against them. The basis of this distinction, or separation, was the blood of the Passover lamb.

> Then Moses called for all the elders of Israel and said to them, "Pick out and take lambs for yourselves according to your families, and kill the Passover lamb. And you shall take a bunch of hyssop, dip it in the blood that is in the basin, and strike the lintel and the two doorposts with the blood that is in the basin. And none of you shall go out of the door of his house until morning. For the LORD will pass through to strike the Egyptians; and when He sees the blood on the lintel and on the two doorposts, the LORD will pass over the

door and not allow the destroyer to come into your houses to strike you."

Exodus 12:21–23

The separation between Israel and Egypt was made by the blood of the lamb when it was displayed on the outside of their homes. Any home that had the blood on the outside was "sanctified." It was set apart to God. No evil power could get into that home because the Lord had made a distinction between His people and those who were not His people through the applied blood of the lamb.

Just as we have done with the other aspects of the work of the blood, we are going to state the appropriate testimony.

> *Through the blood of Jesus, I am sanctified, made holy, set apart to God.*

Please stop your reading at this point and confess this out loud and boldly. You may have had problems feeling that you could never be truly holy no matter how hard you tried. True holiness never comes through keeping rules, controlling ourselves better or trying harder. Holiness comes only through the work of the blood of Jesus on our behalf. Take the hyssop of your testimony, dip it in the blood, and it will do its work. Say it again: *Through the blood of Jesus, I am sanctified, made holy, set apart to God.*

I trust you are beginning to see the power that has been put into our hands as we confess the truth of what the blood does for us. I often say these words: "The devil has no place in me, no power over me, no unsettled claims against me; all has been settled by the blood of Jesus." As we make this our testimony, the power of the blood is released into the spiritual atmosphere around us and things begin to change.

29

Our Physical Bodies

I want to go one step further in relation to the body of the believer. By personal experience, I have learned that it is in our physical bodies where the power of the blood of Jesus really begins to operate. Here is what Scripture says about the body of the believer:

> Do you not know that your body is the temple of the Holy Spirit who is in you, whom you have from God, and you are not your own? For you were bought at a price; therefore glorify God in your body and in your spirit, which are God's.
>
> 1 Corinthians 6:19–20

The phrase *bought at a price* takes us back to the theme of redemption. We have been bought back out of the hand of the devil with the blood of Jesus. How much of us was bought back? Not just our spirit. Our spirit and our body both belong to God because Jesus paid the total redemption price with His blood.

Paul says, therefore, we are to "glorify God" both in our body and in our spirit because both belong to God, redeemed out of the hand of the devil by the blood of Jesus. Neither my spirit, nor my soul, nor my body is under the dominion or control of Satan any longer.

God's Property

Let me state for clarity that I do not believe I have a resurrection body; I have a mortal body. But every fiber, every cell and every tissue of that mortal body is God's property, not the devil's. If, therefore, the enemy comes onto that territory, he is a trespasser. If I correctly understand my rights in Jesus, I can put up a sign that states, "No trespassing—get out!"

Legally my body does not belong to the devil. It belongs to Jesus. Furthermore, Jesus has a special purpose for my body, which is to be the personal residence of the third Person of the Godhead, the Holy Spirit. My body, therefore, is sacred because it is the appointed dwelling place of the Holy Spirit.

Scripture says this clearly: "The Most High does not dwell in temples made with hands" (Acts 7:48; see 1 Kings 8:27; Acts 17:24). God does not live in a church sanctuary or a synagogue. He dwells in a temple that was made by divine workmanship according to divine purpose. He dwells in the body of the believer, redeemed by the blood of Jesus Christ. Paul says, "Foods for the stomach and the stomach for foods, but God will destroy both it and them. Now the body is not for sexual immorality but for the Lord, and the Lord for the body" (1 Corinthians 6:13).

Our physical bodies are not for unclean, immoral purposes. Notice Paul also talks about food for the stomach and the stomach for food. Our bodies are not for sexual immorality nor are they for gluttony.

I have regularly been astonished by this phrase from Proverbs: "The righteous eats to the satisfying of his soul" (Proverbs 13:25). The righteous person does not overeat. Why? Because my body is the Lord's temple, and I am not to defile it by gluttony, drunkenness, immorality or any other misuse.

The body is for the Lord, and the Lord for the body. When I present my body to the Lord, then I have the rights of the Lord for my body. If I purchase a house, I become responsible for its maintenance. If I live in a rented house, however, the landlord is responsible to maintain it. If you merely allow Jesus a kind of temporary or partial right over your body, He does not accept responsibility for the maintenance. If He owns it, however, He is responsible to maintain it—which is the relationship He desires with us. My body is a temple of the Holy Spirit. "The body is for the Lord, the Lord for the body."

Truly Free

This is the foundation for our final testimony, which concerns our bodies. From my experience, I have seen how dynamic this testimony is. People sometimes say to me in a deliverance service, "Brother Prince, how do I know if I'm really free?"

I tell them, "One thing to do is start testifying to the blood." This practice will not work unless the Holy Spirit is present, which we will discuss shortly. If the power of the Spirit of God is in a meeting and people begin to testify to the blood, then I say anything that resists the blood is of Satan. If you continue confessing the blood until there is nothing more inside you that resists, then you can be pretty well assured you are clear.

I have proved this testimony in experience. When you begin to deal with your body, that is when amazing changes start to take place.

Here is our confession:

> *My body is the temple of the Holy Spirit,*
> *redeemed, cleansed, sanctified by the blood of Jesus;*
> *therefore, the devil has no place in me,*
> *and no power over me.*

You might find it a little fearful to say that, thinking all hell is going to turn loose when you challenge the devil in this way. If things start to get stirred up, don't worry! That is a sure sign you have hurt the devil. Just keep on declaring your testimony, and when the storm is cleared, you will find you are still in possession of the territory. Now take a moment to stop and claim, out loud, the work of the blood of Jesus for your physical body.

I remember when I first began to make this kind of testimony. I thought, *Well, I wonder where the devil will hit me next.* I know people who do not testify because they are afraid of what will happen when they do. That is just playing the devil's game. It is his way to keep you from taking a step that is going to put you outside his reach.

Let's counteract that fallacy right now by making the very proclamation we have covered in this chapter:

> *My body is the temple of the Holy Spirit,*
> *redeemed, cleansed, sanctified by the blood of Jesus;*
> *therefore, the devil has no place in me,*
> *and no power over me.*

30

The Blood Speaks in Heaven

There is one more precious and wonderful truth about the blood of Jesus to include in our testimony. It is amazing that many of God's people are totally unaware of this truth.

> But you have come to Mount Zion and to the city of the living God, the heavenly Jerusalem, to an innumerable company of angels, to the general assembly and church of the firstborn who are registered in heaven, to God the Judge of all, to the spirits of just men made perfect, to Jesus the Mediator of the new covenant, and to the blood of sprinkling that speaks better things than that of Abel.
>
> Hebrews 12:22–24

One of the elements in the heavenly Mount Zion is the blood of Jesus, which was sprinkled in the Holy of Holies before the very presence of God on our behalf. After Jesus died on the cross, He entered the Father's presence as our forerunner and representative, having obtained eternal redemption through His blood. When He came before the Father, He sprinkled the evidence of that redemption in the very presence of almighty God the Father. That sprinkled blood "spoke better things than the blood of Abel."

You will remember that early in human history, Cain murdered his brother Abel and then tried to disclaim responsibility before the Lord. But the Lord challenged Cain: "How can you say you don't know where your brother is? The voice of your brother's blood cries out to Me from the ground" (see Genesis 4:10). In so many words God said, "There's no way you can conceal your guilt, because the blood of your brother, which you shed on the earth, is crying out to me for vengeance."

Compare the cry of Abel's blood for vengeance with the blood of Jesus sprinkled in heaven. The blood of Jesus does not cry out for vengeance—it cries out for mercy. The blood of Jesus makes a continual plea in the very presence of God for God's mercy.

Contrast the two cries: the blood of Abel, shed on the earth, cried out for vengeance. The blood of Jesus, sprinkled in heaven, cries out for mercy. I want you to see that once we have testified to the blood of Jesus, making it our own personal testimony, its impact continues. Why? Because the blood of Jesus is speaking continually in the very presence of God on our behalf. Anytime you are troubled, tempted, fearful or anxious, remind yourself of this fact, which is also our next confession:

The blood of Jesus is speaking in God's presence
on my behalf right now.

It is only by the word of your testimony that you get the full benefits of the blood. If you say it once and all hell breaks loose—simply give praise to the Lord and keep saying it. The writer of Hebrews encourages us to hold fast the word of our confession (see Hebrews 4:14). Furthermore, when opposition really turns loose on us, he warns us to hold it fast "without wavering" (Hebrews 10:23). Keep on saying it! It does not depend on your feelings, your situation, your symptoms or your circumstances. Rather, it is as eternally true as the Word of God. It is forever settled in heaven.

The Water and the Blood

Do you truly understand that there is a vital relationship between our testimony of the Word to the blood and the operation of the Holy Spirit? You cannot leave out the Holy Spirit. By testifying to the blood, you bring the Holy Spirit into operation. Speaking of Jesus, 1 John tells us: "This is He who came by water and blood—Jesus Christ; not only by water, but by water and blood. And it is the Spirit who bears witness, because the Spirit is truth" (1 John 5:6).

I will not elaborate, but I understand *the water* to mean the Word of God. Jesus came as the great teacher of the Word of God, sanctifying and cleansing by the washing of water by the Word (see John 15:3; 17:17; Ephesians 5:26). He came as the Great Redeemer, shedding His blood as the redemptive price. These are the two main aspects of His redemptive ministry: redeeming by the blood and cleansing by the washing of water by the Word.

Jesus did not come by the Word only. He did not come as teacher only. He also came as the redemptive Savior to give His life as a ransom for many. This did not set aside His other ministry as teacher. Ephesians 5:26–27 talks of this cleansing role: "That He might sanctify and cleanse her with the washing of water by the word, that He might present her to Himself a glorious church, not having spot or wrinkle or any such thing."

This is the double ministry of Jesus: by the *water of the Word* and by the *shed blood of redemption*.

When we bring the Word and the blood together, therefore, the Spirit of God bears testimony because the Spirit is truth. As you begin to use the Word, stating what the Word says the blood does, the Spirit comes to you and bears testimony to the truth. Without the Holy Spirit this is just religious language. It may be very good language and it may be doctrinally correct. But it does not do anything until the Holy Spirit bears testimony. When the Holy Spirit bears testimony, then it is irresistible.

There are no little rules and regulations in the Christian life that state if you do this, then something automatically works for you. Nothing works without the Holy Spirit. But when you bring the Holy Spirit to work by testifying to the water and the blood, the Spirit bears witness. Then you have three eternal, unchanging forces at work in your behalf: the Word, the blood and the Spirit.

In closing, I want to bring to your attention a little parable in Ecclesiastes 4:12: "A threefold cord is not quickly broken." When you begin to testify to what the Word says the blood does, the Spirit comes to you and you have the threefold cord: the Word, the blood and the Holy Spirit.

I have attached a page at the end of the book that contains each of the testimonies about the work of the blood that we have considered in these last chapters. I encourage you to remove this page and keep it in your Bible or notebook where you may conveniently refer to it and thereby make it part of your frequent and ongoing testimony.

Conclusion

It is my sincere prayer that through what we have covered in this book your vision of spiritual conflict has been expanded and challenged. As I stated in the beginning, we are in a conflict with evil, whether we desire to be so or not. We have only two choices: Either overcome evil, or it will overcome us. It has not been my desire to place fear or dread in your heart through what we have studied. Rather I have hoped to assist you in understanding the battle in which we, as individuals and as the Body of Christ, are engaged.

In so doing, it has been my wish to encourage you that because you are in Christ, and sincerely endeavoring to live daily for Him, you are already a restraining force for good in your environment. Beyond that, I have tried to present the scriptural weapons that I have proved effective through my own life and ministry, and through the experience of countless other believers.

It has always been my effort, as a teacher of the Scriptures to the Body of Christ, not merely to leave people with more knowledge of the Bible, but also to provide practical guidance in effectively applying truth in their daily lives. To that end, I have encouraged you throughout the final chapters of this study to stop and make a practical and personal testimony of truth. I can promise that if you will continually apply these confessions to your life, *you will see changes in your spiritual outlook and in your life.*

Beyond that, I encourage you to think about the challenge God has given you as a disciple of Jesus. How do you see yourself fitting into the struggle against evil in your nation, in your city, in your work or in your family? Are you willing to commit yourself to take a stand to overcome evil with good? If so, I invite you to pray the following prayer, either as I have expressed it or something similar in your own words.

Lord, I thank You that I have been translated out of the dominion of darkness into the Kingdom of Your love. Thank You that through the blood of Jesus, I have been redeemed, forgiven, cleansed, justified, sanctified and delivered from the power of Satan. Thank You that You have given me the weapons by which I am able, by the power of Your Holy Spirit, to overcome evil in my life and to be a part of restraining and casting down Satan's kingdom.

I commit myself, depending upon Your Spirit and Your grace, to overcome evil with good by living in the light of Your Word and trusting in Your love, Your spirit and Your faithfulness. Thank You that You have made me to be salt in a fallen, evil world and that You are working through me, even now, to restrain the powers of darkness and to bring healing and salvation to a lost generation through the weapons You have entrusted to me.

In Your name, Lord Jesus, I cast down all roadblocks to Your truth and victory in my life and in the lives of those around me. I believe that You, through the blood You shed on the cross, have already defeated Satan and won for me the final victory—both now and in eternity.

I thank You now for the victories You will bring, because You are faithful to Your Word! In the name of Jesus, Amen!

My Testimony of the Blood of Jesus

Through the blood of Jesus, I am redeemed out of the hand of the devil.

Through the blood of Jesus, all my sins are forgiven.

As I walk in the light, the blood of Jesus is cleansing me now—and continually—from all sin.

Through the blood of Jesus, I am justified, made righteous, "just-as-if-I'd" never sinned.

Through the blood of Jesus, I am sanctified, made holy, set apart to God.

My body is the temple of the Holy Spirit, redeemed, cleansed, sanctified by the blood of Jesus; therefore, the devil has no place in me, and no power over me.

The blood of Jesus is speaking in God's presence on my behalf right now.

Derek Prince (1915–2003) was born in India of British parents. He was educated as a scholar of Greek and Latin at Eton College and King's College, Cambridge, in England. Upon graduation, he held a fellowship (equivalent to a professorship) in Ancient and Modern Philosophy at King's College. Prince also studied Hebrew, Aramaic and modern languages at Cambridge and the Hebrew University in Jerusalem. As a student, he was a philosopher and a self-proclaimed agnostic.

While serving in the British Medical Corps during World War II, Prince began to study the Bible as a philosophical work. Converted through a powerful encounter with Jesus Christ, he was baptized in the Holy Spirit a few days later. Out of this encounter, he formed two conclusions: first, that Jesus Christ is alive; second, that the Bible is a true, relevant, up-to-date book. These conclusions altered the whole course of his life, which he then devoted to studying and teaching the Bible as the Word of God.

Derek's main gift of explaining the Bible and its teaching, in a clear and simple way, has helped build a foundation of faith in millions of lives. His non-denominational, non-sectarian approach has made his teaching equally relevant and helpful to people from all racial and religious backgrounds.

He is the author of more than 80 books, 600 audio and 110 video teachings, many of which have been translated and published in more than 100 languages. His daily radio broadcast, which began in 1979, is translated into Arabic, Bahasa (Indonesia), Chinese (Amoy, Cantonese, Mandarin, Shanghaiese, Swatow), Croatian, German, Malagasy, Mongolian, Russian, Samoan, Spanish and Tongan. The radio program continues today to touch lives around the world.

Derek Prince Ministries persists in reaching out to believers in more than 140 countries with Derek's teaching, fulfilling the mandate to keep on "until Jesus returns." This is accomplished through the outreaches of more than 45 Derek Prince offices around the world, including primary work in Australia, Canada, China, France, Germany, the Netherlands, New Zealand, Norway, Russia, South Africa, Switzerland, the United Kingdom and the United States. For current information about these and other worldwide locations, visit www.derekprince.com.